Praise for *Are We Happy Yet?*

"In her inspiring book, *Are We Happy Yet? Eight Keys to Unlocking a Joyful Life,* Lisa Cypers Kamen delightfully shares her enthusiasm for the happiness that resides within each of us. She offers the reader an opportunity to remember how to let their light shine and practical keys for doing so!"

—**H. Ronald Hulnick PhD, and Mary R. Hulnick PhD,**
authors of *Loyalty to Your Soul: The Heart of Spiritual Psychology*

"Lisa Cypers Kamen is a master of positive thinking, and she's on a mission to make the world a happier place—person by person . . . starting with you. The book is neatly organized around eight keys, and readers who feel they want more out of life but aren't sure how to get it are likely to find at least one key to unlock the secrets of happiness that have eluded them."

—**Stan Tatkin, PsyD, MFT,**
author of *Wired for Love*

"Lisa Cypers Kamen blends a wellspring of professional experience, research, and tales from her personal school of hard knocks to demonstrate how and why our personal happiness not only really matters but is within our personal power to create. Follow the robust user-friendly eight keys contained within *Are We Happy Yet?* and you will find yourself happier for having done so."

—**Christine Hassler,**
author of *Expectation Hangover: Overcoming Disappointment in Work, Love, and Life*

"Lisa speaks about happiness and courageous living while compelling us to listen. She knows how to overcome adversity and has gone beyond boundaries to reach us with compassion, trust, and fearless vision by challenging us to be responsible for creating happiness no matter what life brings. We can accomplish amazing things with greater courage, optimism, and intentional actions. She inspires me and all those she reaches with her wisdom."

—**Agapi Stassinopoulos,**
author of *Unbinding the Heart*

"For those who find happiness to be elusive, this book is a perfect road map. I recommend it wholeheartedly."

—**Arun Gandhi,**
president of Gandhi Worldwide Education Institute and author of *Grandfather Gandhi* and *Be the Change*

"Do you want to be happier? If so, be kind to yourself and read this book. It's loaded with practical, no-nonsense tips, and tools that will that will help guide you to a happier version of yourself."

—**Michele Borba, EdD,**
author of *Unselfie: Why Empathetic Kids Succeed in Our All-About-Me World*

"For skeptics and seekers, Lisa Cypers Kamen challenges us to explore where happiness really lives, especially after hardship. *Are We Happy Yet?* delivers a factual and practical approach with heart and humor to support anyone seeking a more empowered approach to life."

—**Michelle Gielan,**
author of *Broadcasting Happiness*

"In all of her endeavors and life study, Lisa poses the ultimate question that many are asking: Are We Happy Yet? Lisa shows you exactly how to transform your daily life into your bliss. This book pleasantly acts as a guide for the human being who doesn't wish to settle for anything less—but to wake up and feel inspired and in joy every single day. I know you'll enjoy this read!"

—**Kristine Carlson,**
coauthor of the *Don't Sweat the Small Stuff* book series

"*Are We Happy Yet?* offers self-help in the truest and most positive sense: that of self-mastery. Through a series of surprisingly simple and practical steps Lisa Cypers Kamen guides us to raise what she calls our 'happiness quotient.' "

—**Gabor Maté, MD,**
author of *In the Realm of Hungry Ghosts: Close Encounters with Addiction*

"How to help people help themselves is both an art and a science. Lisa Cypers Kamen has captured both with her cheerful but skilled interactive exercises in a book about happiness—and who wouldn't want to help themselves to achieve it."

—**Jimmie Holland, MD,**
coauthor of *Lighter as We Go: Virtues, Character Strengths, and Aging*

"We spend our lives in pursuit of happiness and Lisa Cypers Kamen helps us go back to its source—ourselves. I highly recommend reading this book if you are looking for tools for leading a happier life."

—**Tiffany Shlain,**
Emmy-nominated filmmaker and founder of Character Day

"In a world that seems to print only bad news, where friendships are virtual, and therefore too often without meaning, Lisa Cypers Kamen is a tonic for the weary soul. Kamen's essential insight is in the tradition of the revered Abraham Lincoln who reminded us that 'most folks can be happy if they just set their mind to be.' "

—**Douglas W. Kmiec,**
author of *Lift Up Your Hearts*

HAPPINESS WAITS FOR
NO ONE...

Are We HAPPY Yet?

Are We HAPPY Yet?

New Revised Edition

Eight Keys to Unlocking a Joyful Life

LISA CYPERS KAMEN

Dragon Gypsy Inc. Publishing

Dragon Gypsy Inc. Publishing
2934 Beverly Glen Circle
Suite 371
Los Angeles, CA 90077
www.DragonGypsyPublishing.com
Email: info@DragonGypsyPublishing.com

For foreign and translation rights, contact Nigel J. Yorwerth
Email: nigel@PublishingCoaches.com

Library of Congress Control Number: 2016916569

ISBN: 978-0-9962131-3-4 (paperback)
ISBN: 978-0-9962131-1-0 (e-book)

10 9 8 7 6 5 4 3 2 1

Cover design by Miladinka Milic
Book design by Vladimir Zavgorodny

Printed in the United States of America

Disclaimer: The purpose of this book is to educate, delight, provoke, and entertain. Its contents are not a substitute for medical, clinical, or psychological treatment. Neither the author nor the publisher guarantees the outcome of the tips, techniques, or information contained herein, and they have neither liability nor responsibility to anyone for any claim of loss or damage caused or alleged to be caused, directly or indirectly, by the information contained in this book.

Some names and identifying details in the stories and examples in this book have been changed to protect the privacy of individuals.

Dedication

"For a seed to achieve its greatest expression, it must come completely undone. The shell cracks, its insides come out and everything changes. To someone who does not understand personal growth, it would look like complete destruction."

~ Cynthia Occelli ~

For my clients . . . in honor and celebration of your courageous hearts and curious minds that lead you onto your paths of discovery, healing, and joy. Heartfelt gratitude to the valiant military service personnel who serve our country and return home invisibly wounded. You need not suffer in silence or solitude. Thank you for allowing me to bear witness to and support your transformations. You touch my soul with hope, belief, and optimism . . . in all ways and always.

"It is not the answer that enlightens, but the question."

~ Eugène Ionesco ~

Contents

Ding dong.
Your happiness awaits.

Open the door
and invite it in.

Foreword

I first met Lisa Kamen at my home in Portland, Oregon. She arrived on a typically rainy afternoon with her daughter and camera equipment in tow. Lisa was in the midst of realizing a dream: she was making a movie about happiness. In a world where everyone from my postal worker to the guy at the deli seems to have an idea for a screenplay it was refreshing to see Lisa making this dream a reality. What's more, she was using this extraordinary opportunity as a means of showing her daughter the world. Lisa was traveling around the United States and abroad asking people about their happiness. As a happiness researcher myself I believe that Lisa's work is both important and instructive.

Make no mistake, I sometimes feel a degree of territoriality that comes with professional expertise. Like many academics I can feel my feathers getting ruffled when someone comes along and offers their armchair view on the complicated architecture of happiness. It is, however, people exactly like Lisa who have turned around my attitude. In every subsequent meeting with Lisa I have been reminded of her deep well of humanity—donating money to schools, serving others, doting on her children and helping our returning soldiers and their families challenged by Combat Stress restore their smiles and thrive through Harvesting Happiness for Heroes. I have come to realize that voices like Lisa's are not just tolerable in the public conversation on happiness, but welcome. By virtue of her media—Internet radio broadcast, film, and popular writing—and through her breadth of experience, Lisa offers new insights into living the Good Life.

Many of these ideas you will—fortunately—find in the pages of this book. To name just a single example, Lisa does a clever job of describing the relationship between "having more" and "having less" of a commodity such as time or money. She throws conventional thinking to the wind and offers a more complex view of these psychological leanings. It is not that having more is better and having less is worse. Lisa challenges us all to look at the balancing act between more and less. I will leave it for you to discover in the pages ahead exactly how to do this. This book is full of these types of gems and I hope you are as affected by Lisa's positive contribution to the world as I am.

~ **Robert Biswas-Diener, PhD**
Managing Director, Positive Acorn
Portland, Oregon

Introduction

"The way to find out about happiness is to keep your mind on those moments when you feel most happy—not excited, not just thrilled, but deeply happy. This requires a little bit of self-analysis. What is it that makes you happy? Stay with it, no matter what people tell you. This is what is called following your bliss."

~ Joseph Campbell ~

If I were to ask you what makes you happy, would you be able to answer? Don't worry if you could not. You're not the only one who's struggling right now to find your happiness, and how can you find it if you don't quite know what it looks like? All you know is this:

Things don't feel right and you need to do something about it.

You might be thinking that you've already done everything you were supposed to do to be happy: you played by the rules, you went to school, you got married, you had kids. But no matter what you have attained and achieved, there is something that is still missing. But what? You have no idea how to seek it out and find it, and maybe no clear vision of what to do with it should you happen to stumble upon it.

For the time being, you have continued to do the things that everyone else does to make their lives happier: you make money, buy new things, read books, watch movies, take classes, try to get to the gym, lose weight, and focus on "self-improvement" through external means.

And still, you are not quite happy. The outside environment you have surrounded yourself with is not taking care of the inside job of bringing you any lasting happiness.

Maybe you even built your company, married a fantastic mate, and now drive the car of your childhood dreams. But every day you still wake up with the feeling that there should be something more to your life. Some days you can avoid that feeling, while other days it lingers around the edges of your thoughts and registers in your emotions as a sense of discomfort or dissatisfaction.

For all of us, things would be so much easier if achieving the great American dream would fulfill us inside. If things really happened the way they do in the movies.

But what happens after the credits fade?

What does happily ever after actually look like?

The answer to this is something I've come to understand. I'm not different than most people in that I've endured a lot of unwelcome events in my life, fighting against them despite their being unavoidable—they were going to happen whether I wanted them to or not.

Beginning back in 2008 and continuing through 2012, I had what most would agree was a streak of really lousy luck. My ex-husband and I separated, he was hospitalized, we lost homes and investment properties resulting from the recession and he was forced into bankruptcy. Then, at the end of 2012 I had an additional financial upheaval when my employer quite literally dropped dead. My children and I became functionally homeless. All that was horrible, of course, and it was made even worse by the fact that I no longer had financial reserves, a place to call home, or child support for my two children.

Needless to say, it took all my resources to stay upright. I could not afford to indulge in a "pity party" no matter how "well deserved" it might seem to be. Fortunately, I'd already been working with happiness as a career so I had some knowledge and information about how to manage my attitude and deal with my emotions and help my children do the same. My two preteens were depending on me for all manner of support. The life that we'd known was suddenly gone. Poof! The only thing I could do to regain a portion of what we'd lost was to use my resources and try to create something new. Dare I say—something better! Failure was not an option.

These life challenges were not just about me either or my children. There was the heartbreak and determination to help a formerly drug-addicted close family member that compelled me as well as an ex-husband who had daily struggles with mental illness. All of these things impacted me although they were not specifically mine to manage.

Other peoples' problems can definitely feel like our problems. Because it is only through connection and community that we become whole, healed, and at home. But while the people in our lives do impact the flow of our activity each and every day, it's up to us to make sure this flow moves in a favorable direction that works for us while also serving others. We all have to "pass" on the victim mentality because it is one thing in life that we can't afford and that we actually *can* control and avoid. If you want to be happy, avoid victimhood at all costs.

Are We Happy Yet? is all about the transformative power of self-mastery. Enjoy the journey and the process of becoming the hero of your own life.

~ Lisa Cypers Kamen

Getting Past the Past

All of us are shaped to varying degrees by our pasts. That is unavoidable. But we do not have to be defined by our history. While we all have emotional baggage, we can either let it weigh us down or use it as a catalyst to transform ourselves.

The journey of coming home to one's self is a powerful one, and it's definitely not boring! Is it smooth and uneventful? No way! But each thing that comes our way is an opportunity to learn, grow, and move toward a better life. It's also a chance to live by example for those whom we want to positively influence—our children, our peers, and even strangers who simply "take note" of what we're doing.

A friend of mine whose car was totaled in what could have been a fatal accident was "reduced" to taking the bus all over town for two years. She chose to make this more interesting for herself by holding the intention to be like one of the angelic characters in the then-popular TV show *Touched by an Angel.* On one occasion, she was sitting next to a fellow who was watching with amusement an inebriated woman repeatedly fall asleep and then jerk awake just as her head was about to strike a metal railing due to the bouncing of the bus. The man was waiting for the "inevitable" bonk on the head as if he was watching an entertaining TV show. My friend, on the other hand, got up out of the seat and sat down next to the dozing woman so that if her bobbling head should lean too close to the railing, that her shoulder would be there to protect her from getting hurt. And that's precisely what happened. The reason I bring this up is because in her desire to set an example of compassion for others, she created a lasting memory of loving service for herself that never fails to fill her with good feelings when she recalls it.

My own desire to serve others in their quest to create a thriving life is how I have chosen to transform my own painful adversity into greater happiness and well-being. I've found that when there is an alignment of passion, purpose, place, and meaning in how we live our lives, new doors open. We begin to experience life as a more hospitable journey in spite of its many challenges.

Humans are social creatures. We are hard-wired to connect, love, and belong to and with one another. Often we've been hurt and disappointed by painful past events that lead us to retreat, isolate, and disconnect from the very things that makes life worth living—our relationships. What if our lives have been filled with challenge, trauma and darkness?

Endeavoring to transform ourselves can be daunting. Yet for some it becomes the only worthy path because the lives we have been living have grown so uncomfortable that the only viable option is to confront and heal the roots of the perpetual pain and suffering.

It's important to point out that all of us experience resistance to change—to varying degrees—even though we may know it's good for us. Change takes us out of our comfort zone and our comfort zone is "the devil we have come to know." But our comfort zone is also where dreams go to die. Former Prime Minister of South Africa P.W. Botha once said, "we must adapt or die."

So herein lies our challenge, to choose and implement change because the positive benefits of doing so outweigh the negative cost of doing the same thing over and over again without achieving a rewarding result. But in order to change we must shift our perspective from our perceived brokenness to focusing attention, intention, and action towards improving our resilience, grit, hardiness, guts, chutzpah, strength-of-heart, and perseverance in pursuit of meaning-making and noble purpose in our lives.

In the 15th century, the Japanese originated an ancient art process to repair broken pottery called *kintsukuroi*. Literally, this means to repair with gold. The Japanese belief behind this word is that the true life of a piece begins the moment it is damaged. Once broken, it has the potential to offer a renewed sense of beauty, vitality, and history because of its past. It is therefore repaired with precious metals and other materials that celebrate the cracks rather than attempt to disguise them.

As author, singer, songwriter Leonard Cohen puts it, "There is a crack in everything. That is how the light gets in."

The idea that we can become more beautiful because of the ways we have been hurt is the inspiration behind the eight keys to unlocking a joyful life at the heart of this new, revised edition.

What does it take to achieve sustainable well-being and a happier life? It takes practice and also a healthy dose of self-education. And yes, it takes commitment, as well. But the results make it all worthwhile, for they can leave us feeling full and more satisfied than we may have ever thought possible. I know! I'm living proof that the eight keys to unlocking a joyful life work. I use each and every one of them for I am choosing to thrive rather than merely to survive.

The intention behind this book is to debunk the annoying yellow "smiley face" notion of happiness. Happiness isn't an icon that you insert at the end of a sentence. It is a way of life, a flourishing existence defined by fulfillment, growth, and contentment. Truly, it is a hero's journey that many will take, and many more should!

Happiness is not instant gratification, although sometimes it helps. And it doesn't have to be fleeting. It requires attention, intention, and action. But so does anything worth having. Happiness is emotional muscle-tone that is: soul-centered, heart-focused, authentically, intimately, interdependent and interconnected.

You're going to find wisdom and practical steps that stem from the heart of experience, not from the research of a scholar, and this is intentionally so. It's a gentle read, written in everyday language for regular people although my words are all grounded in science.

Every story has a story. I did not wander into my happy place. There was a personal evolution to my happiness revolution born from living life on life's terms. One does not reach the light without having traveled through the dark. I realize there is value in sharing my story as well as those of others and will include it along with the scientific theories that are the foundation of my work.

In this newly revised edition of this book, I hope you will find some of your answers—the keys that will help you unlock the happiness you have always desired—which awaits you within. It takes time to recognize that we deserve to feel good—no matter what. Recalling the words of two of my favorite graduate school professors, "it's never the issue that's the issue, it's our relationship to the issue that's the issue."

Progress is a gift that comes through effort. And progress is not always linear. We can feel as though we are working our butts off and not getting anywhere and then suddenly one day when we least expect it—there is a shift. I encourage you to approach your own exploration of happiness like a curious adventurer in search of something new, pleasurable, and just slightly outside of your comfort zone because that is where growth happens.

"It does not matter how slowly you go as long as you do not stop".

~ *Confucius* ~

Universally User-Friendly Principles for Humankind

As we grow up, we all harbor both public and secret dreams. Over the years, however, we often let go of those dreams for many reasons. Sometimes, we're made to feel selfish for even having held these dreams, and sometimes we censor ourselves. Have you ever said this to yourself: "Who am I to be dreaming of this? This will never happen to me. I should just forget about it, and be realistic." It's as if we're not allowed to have these dreams.

Here are some basic realities: Often we dream of doing things, even big things, and feel as though it's totally possible. Other times those dreams are not fully realistic; they need to be tweaked or reworked. Perhaps, they will one day be realistic, but somewhere down the road. Making dreams come true requires placing attention, intention, and actions in the directions of those goals. Timing is also an important and often mysterious factor.

"Don't judge each day by the harvest you reap,
but by the seeds you plant."

~ *Robert Louis Stevenson* ~

The reason these words resonate within me is because I believe it takes great courage to change. I also appreciate this old adage: "it's not what happens to us, but how we react that makes the difference." We can cower and hide away when some of our dreams fail to come true. Then again, we can sit down over a hot cup of tea and ask ourselves how we can best deal with the situation. By asking ourselves powerful open-ended questions such as "What has this experience taught me?" or "What am I meant to learn from this?" we can reframe and transform our perceptions. Each experience in life can teach us something if we're willing to learn.

In order to flourish in life, we must first embrace the concept that everyone in this world is interconnected and interdependent. While we may live a seemingly independent life, we are dependent on all sorts of people we never will meet—like those who grow the food we eat, those who package and market it, those who drive it to our grocery store, etc., etc. When we recognize our interdependence, the process of giving and receiving help heighten our awareness of our place in the intricate web of life. This is in direct opposition to the ethos of the Baby "me generation" Boomers that support entitlement, self-righteous indignation, trusting no one except yourself, seeking instant gratification, and a whole host of self-involved narcissism that negates cooperation and collaboration and supports looking out for #1 at the expense of others. Our whole quality of life and the future of our species have been jeopardized by that very attitude when held by those at the helm of corporate and political entities.

What I am suggesting is personal accountability and behavioral health combined with collective social responsibility for the greater good. Living in a United States of Inter-Dependence is a lot less stressful as we create a community of people with whom we can work for many different purposes. The notion of interconnectivity is not new, of course. The "green movement" promotes the notion of a healthy planet based on the belief that we are all interconnected—all of the ecosystems, all of the different species, and humanity, as well.

In order to live by universal principles, we must be willing to let go of the notion that we can control all the outcomes in our life. We replace this illusion with the universal operating principles for living the "good life" and developing virtuous character. They include:

- Honesty
- Vulnerability
- Forgiveness
- Inspiration
- Integrity
- Passion
- Compassion
- Authenticity

These are beautiful intentions to hold, but how do we make them real in our life? Here are some tips for things you can do right now to live by these universal principles more and more each day:

1. **Create balance**
    - There are four aspects that affect your life: the mental, emotional, spiritual, and physical domains. As you begin to create greater balance amongst these four aspects, then you will find greater peace and contentment in everyday life. Entertain the possibility of working with the 8

bullet-pointed virtuous character principles listed above. Ask yourself: "How can I bring these principles into my life?" Then proceed to list 2-3 ways in which you can fully integrate these principles in a practical way.
- Focus on letting go of thoughts, judgments, and behaviors that do not positively serve you. Write down 2-5 aspects of your life that you feel you need to control, and how you can let go of that need and work with the principle of balance.

2. **Capture the moment, let go of regret and negative future-tripping**

When something (or someone) attracts your interest, why not capture the moment by journaling how you feel about it? Then, you can take action steps to pursue it when the time is right. All too often we're either stuck in regrets about the past . . . or fears of the future. Imagine how it would feel to live fully in the moment. Here is a process that can help you bring that possibility to life for yourself.

- Write down 2-3 regrets you have about the past. Now, either take them to a large body of water and let them slip away, or burn them—safely, of course! Then tell yourself, "I give myself permission to fully let go." Do the same with 2-3 fears about the future.
- Write down 2-3 ways you prevent yourself from living in the present. Now, write down 2-3 strategies you can create for changing this pattern. Keep them in an open space where you can see them and connect with them on a regular basis.
- Practice and repeat as needed.

3. Move it or lose it = exercise

You will learn a lot about yourself while you are working out as well as from other people engaged in similar physical activities. You can make friends or just simply observe other individuals. Either way this is another activity in which we connect with our bodies in health and with others in community. By the way, just being out in nature and moving our body will boost our mind. Here are some alternatives if you feel that the gym just isn't for you:

- Swimming
- Nature walking/hiking
- Walking with friends
- Yoga
- Tai Chi
- Bike riding

Any of these would be a healthy habit to pick up, and your heart will love and thank you for it.

Discovering Your Happiness-Factor

"The key to growth is the introduction of consciousness into our awareness."

~ Lao Tzu ~

This is the starting point—the introduction to a new, more organic way of approaching life! Through this beginning exercise, you can deconstruct the puzzle of your life. It's time to put together the jigsaw pieces of your past that until now may have been scattered around the rooms of your mind, and to spur the thought processes that will help you discover and cultivate your inner-happiness.

Keep in mind that becoming happy is not a one-day rush job, but rather a slow, meticulous, and deep assessment of your past and future life, your thought processes, and how you may have been sabotaging your own happiness in the past—oftentimes, unknowingly!

Discovering your *H-Factor* is a means to uncovering our authenticity and showing up for life by giving ourselves full permission to experience unadulterated joy rather than simply to avoid pain. This is a learning tool to begin to examine how your life has "evolved" and how you have grown—or not grown—as a person. Taking an honest and intimate look at your reflection in the mirror will help you sort through and organize your life-altering events and patterns. By doing this, you will begin sowing seeds of greater awareness. And with awareness comes consciousness through which we can begin to shift, change, grow, and transform. When we tend to our own garden, we can cultivate a beautiful harvest.

To harvest a thriving garden we need healthy seeds, the right amount of light and water, and regular nurturing to ensure that all goes well. This book, as well as your desire, will support you in this process.

Your *H-Factor* is the set-point or default setting of happiness or unhappiness you will always return to no matter what good or bad things happen to you. If your *H-Factor* is low, it is probably partially genetic, and you will have to work harder than people with a higher *H-Factor* in order to reach and maintain an optimum level of happiness. If your *H-Factor* is high, you are one of those lucky people who were born with a genetic happiness-advantage. Life circumstances may get you down, but you always rise back to your high level of natural happiness. It's important to note that happy people do not experience less trauma, stress, disappointment, or loss in their lives than unhappy people. However, happy people have a greater tolerance to distress and possess an innate ability to bounce back more easily after bad things happen. Happy people are resilient people.

Regardless of your pre-wired set-point, there are proven ways to alter, elevate, and reboot your *H-Factor*, starting right now.

Defining Your H-Factor

Through self-knowledge, we gain personal power to make better choices and to better understand where our natural and habitual thought processes stem from. For some, this may seem like a startling endeavor, but please realize that you should welcome it. Once you know the facts about "you," there is an abundance of opportunity to enrich your internal soil so you can begin cultivating more happiness.

It's time to pinpoint your *H-Factor*. Is it low, medium, or high?

Mark the number that best describes your answer to each question:

1. How often do you look for the positive in what initially seems like a negative experience?

① Never ② Rarely ③ Sometimes ④ Often ⑤ Always

2. Do you tend to overreact to situations that others might find annoying but not traumatic?

⑤ Never ④ Rarely ③ Sometimes ② Often ① Always

3. If things are going too well for you do you tell yourself that you don't deserve it?

⑤ Never ④ Rarely ③ Sometimes ② Often ① Always

4. Do you sabotage your life through habitually finding fault with everyone and everything?

⑤ Never ④ Rarely ③ Sometimes ② Often ① Always

5. How often do you experience a sense of well-being?

① Never ② Rarely ③ Sometimes ④ Often ⑤ Always

6. How often do you feel sad for no particular reason?

⑤ Never ④ Rarely ③ Sometimes ② Often ① Always

7. Do you ever feel shy or socially awkward?

⑤ Never ④ Rarely ③ Sometimes ② Often ① Always

8. Do you feel like you are on the outside looking in?

⑤ Never ④ Rarely ③ Sometimes ② Often ① Always

9. Do you ever feel that something is basically wrong with you?

⑤ Never ④ Rarely ③ Sometimes ② Often ① Always

10. Do you feel something is wrong with your life?

⑤ Never ④ Rarely ③ Sometimes ② Often ① Always

11. Do you feel others are happier or have a better life than you do?

⑤ Never ④ Rarely ③ Sometimes ② Often ① Always

12. Do you feel like you are a victim of someone or something?

⑤ Never ④ Rarely ③ Sometimes ② Often ① Always

13. Do you have a sense of purpose?

① Never ② Rarely ③ Sometimes ④ Often ⑤ Always

14. Do you get frustrated easily?

⑤ Never ④ Rarely ③ Sometimes ② Often ① Always

15. Do your feelings get hurt easily?

⑤ Never ④ Rarely ③ Sometimes ② Often ① Always

16. Do you think the best of everyone unless you find out otherwise?

① Never ② Rarely ③ Sometimes ④ Often ⑤ Always

17. Do you think most people have bad intentions?

⑤ Never ④ Rarely ③ Sometimes ② Often ① Always

18. Do you try to give people the benefit of the doubt?

① Never ② Rarely ③ Sometimes ④ Often ⑤ Always

19. Do you feel good about how you look?

① Never ② Rarely ③ Sometimes ④ Often ⑤ Always

20. Are there things about your body that you hate?

⑤ Never ④ Rarely ③ Sometimes ② Often ① Always

21. Do you try to improve the things about your body you don't like?

① Never ② Rarely ③ Sometimes ④ Often ⑤ Always

22. Do you have mood swings?

⑤ Never ④ Rarely ③ Sometimes ② Often ① Always

23. Do you get angry or upset easily?

⑤ Never ④ Rarely ③ Sometimes ② Often ① Always

24. Can you feel contentment and appreciation even if things are not going well for you?

① Never ② Rarely ③ Sometimes ④ Often ⑤ Always

25. Do you feel unhappy or depressed about even small setbacks?

⑤ Never ④ Rarely ③ Sometimes ② Often ① Always

26. Do you smile a lot?

① Never ② Rarely ③ Sometimes ④ Often ⑤ Always

27. Is your smile always genuine?

① Never ② Rarely ③ Sometimes ④ Often ⑤ Always

28. Do you cry easily?

⑤ Never ④ Rarely ③ Sometimes ② Often ① Always

29. Do you seek out fun new and exciting experiences?

① Never ② Rarely ③ Sometimes ④ Often ⑤ Always

30. Do you wait for others to motivate you to do something?

⑤ Never ④ Rarely ③ Sometimes ② Often ① Always

31. Do you ever think unhappy thoughts?

⑤ Never ④ Rarely ③ Sometimes ② Often ① Always

32. Do you worry about unimportant things?

⑤ Never ④ Rarely ③ Sometimes ② Often ① Always

33. Do you feel optimistic about your life?

① Never ② Rarely ③ Sometimes ④ Often ⑤ Always

34. Do you feel disappointed about your life?

⑤ Never ④ Rarely ③ Sometimes ② Often ① Always

35. Do you believe that you *deserve* a happy life?

① Never ② Rarely ③ Sometimes ④ Often ⑤ Always

36. Are you enjoying your life?
① Never ② Rarely ③ Sometimes ④ Often ⑤ Always

37. Are you enjoying your work?
① Never ② Rarely ③ Sometimes ④ Often ⑤ Always

38. Do you need to buy things to make you happy?
⑤ Never ④ Rarely ③ Sometimes ② Often ① Always

39. Do you love yourself?
① Never ② Rarely ③ Sometimes ④ Often ⑤ Always

40. Do you forgive yourself?
① Never ② Rarely ③ Sometimes ④ Often ⑤ Always

41. Do you forgive others?
① Never ② Rarely ③ Sometimes ④ Often ⑤ Always

42. Are you the kind of person you would like as a friend?
① Never ② Rarely ③ Sometimes ④ Often ⑤ Always

43. Do you focus on your flaws and shortcomings?
⑤ Never ④ Rarely ③ Sometimes ② Often ① Always

44. Do you focus on the flaws and shortcomings of others?
⑤ Never ④ Rarely ③ Sometimes ② Often ① Always

45. Do you feel you must be perfect?
⑤ Never ④ Rarely ③ Sometimes ② Often ① Always

46. Do you dwell on your problems?
⑤ Never ④ Rarely ③ Sometimes ② Often ① Always

47. Do you see your problems as exciting challenges and growth opportunities?

① Never ② Rarely ③ Sometimes ④ Often ⑤ Always

48. Do you do something every day to make someone else happy?

① Never ② Rarely ③ Sometimes ④ Often ⑤ Always

49. Are you ready to let go of preconceived ideas about how your life should be?

① Never ② Rarely ③ Sometimes ④ Often ⑤ Always

50. Do you feel guilty?

① Never ② Rarely ③ Sometimes ④ Often ⑤ Always

51. How often do you feel forgiveness toward those who may have hurt or harmed you or someone you love?

① Never ② Rarely ③ Sometimes ④ Often ⑤ Always

52. Do you feel lethargic and that everything is a chore?

⑤ Never ④ Rarely ③ Sometimes ② Often ① Always

53. Do you manage your own expectations?

① Never ② Rarely ③ Sometimes ④ Often ⑤ Always

54. Do you accept the passage of time and aging with grace?

① Never ② Rarely ③ Sometimes ④ Often ⑤ Always

55. Do you live in the *now*?

① Never ② Rarely ③ Sometimes ④ Often ⑤ Always

56. Do you think loving, kind thoughts about others?

① Never ② Rarely ③ Sometimes ④ Often ⑤ Always

57. Do you think loving, kind thoughts about *yourself*?

① Never ② Rarely ③ Sometimes ④ Often ⑤ Always

58. Do you ever have mean thoughts? (Be honest. We all do sometimes.)

⑤ Never ④ Rarely ③ Sometimes ② Often ① Always

59. Do you try to find the good in everyone and everything?

① Never ② Rarely ③ Sometimes ④ Often ⑤ Always

60. Do you try to focus on what is good in your life?

① Never ② Rarely ③ Sometimes ④ Often ⑤ Always

61. Do you believe that there is enough abundance to go around for everyone?

① Never ② Rarely ③ Sometimes ④ Often ⑤ Always

62. Do you feel jealous (threatened by others) and envious (wanting what someone else has)?

⑤ Never ④ Rarely ③ Sometimes ② Often ① Always

63. Do you feel sorry for yourself?

⑤ Never ④ Rarely ③ Sometimes ② Often ① Always

64. Do you hang out with happy people?

① Never ② Rarely ③ Sometimes ④ Often ⑤ Always

65. Do you have emotionally toxic people in your life?

⑤ Never ④ Rarely ③ Sometimes ② Often ① Always

Score your *H-Factor*

Add up the numbers next to your answers and find out where your *H-Factor* is. From there, the pathway to more authentic happiness begins!

280-325 **Very High**

You are blessed with a very high *H-Factor,* which means that you are a naturally happy person. If you do feel unhappy sometimes, or even now, it means that it is probably situationally-based and will lift once you resolve the unhappy situation.

211-279 **High**

You are usually happy, but you could be happier at times. While your outlook on life is usually positive, life's ups and downs can get to you and make you feel less optimistic than you would like to be. Work on your attitudes and reactions to the people and events in your life, learning to let go of toxic people and stress-producing situations. You will find some great insights in this book on how you can do that.

161-210 **Average** ✓

You are happy sometimes, but not nearly as much as you would like to be or could be. Lots of things bother you and you tend to over-internalize and over-analyze the people and events in your life. As mentioned earlier, much of your unhappiness is not based on what happens in your life, but how you perceive what happens in your life. Use some of the suggestions in this book to work on reacting less to situations and upsetting people. Choose to focus more on improving the quality of your life through your work, by improving your health and fitness, and by helping others.

100-160 **Low**

Raising your *H-Factor* is very possible even if it is low and you are genetically less happy or just unhappy about the way your life is going right now. You will find many ways to change your attitudes and thought processes about your life in this book. Work on smiling more, being more thankful, meeting new people, and doing more "fun" things in your life. Decide that you *deserve* to derive more pleasure from your life. This is a journey marked by progress not perfection, and change results from continual intentional practice to make new habits become permanent routines.

66 to 99 **Very Low**

If your *H-Factor* is very low, it means that you are probably genetically or biologically predisposed to be less happy than some other people. You may also have endured severe abuse or trauma of another kind. Perhaps you are depressed. You must work harder consistently to be happy than those who are blessed with more "happy hormones." One of the blessings in all this is the depth of empathy you can develop for other people and yourself. Reprogramming your inner-thoughts may be a challenge for you, but you can do it if you are constantly aware of your negative thoughts and change them by regularly practicing more productive, kind, loving, and positive thoughts. Remember, practice makes permanent.

By uncovering where we presently sit on the *H-Factor* scale, we can more honestly assess and take responsibility for the journey that led us to this moment. Exciting possibilities of transformation and transcendence are waiting to welcome us through this journey.

"Happiness is a choice that requires effort at times."

~ *Aeschylus* ~

The Positive Currency Bank

Most of us would agree that having money provides a sense of security thus contributing to our happiness. However, money itself cannot buy happiness. Happiness is an emotion and sensibility that manifests from the generation of positive social currency by you and those around you. Take inventory on *How Much Positive Currency is in Your Happiness Bank?* This test will show you how much positive emotional currency you have in your capital reserve account.

Mark the number that best describes your answer to each question:

1. Do you do consciously do something to make others smile every day?

① Never ② Rarely ③ Sometimes ④ Often ⑤ Always

2. Do you do something that brings you pleasure every day?

① Never ② Rarely ③ Sometimes ④ Often ⑤ Always

3. Do you bestow sincere compliments every day and often?

① Never ② Rarely ③ Sometimes ④ Often ⑤ Always

4. Do you receive compliments gracefully and graciously?

① Never ② Rarely ③ Sometimes ④ Often ⑤ Always

5. Do you take an active interest in others' successes as well as challenges?

① Never ② Rarely ③ Sometimes ④ Often ⑤ Always

6. Do you practice acts of random kindness by doing something good for someone else anonymously?

① Never ② Rarely ③ Sometimes ④ Often ⑤ Always

7. Do you focus on what is right with your life, not on what is wrong with it?

① Never ② Rarely ③ Sometimes ④ Often ⑤ Always

8. Do you acknowledge that the world can be a harsh, difficult and unfair place and then refuse to let it get you down?

① Never ② Rarely ③ Sometimes ④ Often ⑤ Always

9. Have you become your own best friend by learning to understand yourself and your needs?

① Never ② Rarely ③ Sometimes ④ Often ⑤ Always

10. Do you take control of your own life and accept responsibility for your own happiness?

① Never ② Rarely ③ Sometimes ④ Often ⑤ Always

11. Have you developed a sense of worth by doing something good for society?

① Never ② Rarely ③ Sometimes ④ Often ⑤ Always

12. Have you become self-sufficient?

① Never ② Rarely ③ Sometimes ④ Often ⑤ Always

13. Have you made doing for others as important as doing for yourself?

① Never ② Rarely ③ Sometimes ④ Often ⑤ Always

14. Can you find humor in most situations, even very difficult ones?

① Never ② Rarely ③ Sometimes ④ Often ⑤ Always

15. Do you see adversity as a challenge from which you can learn and grow?

① Never ② Rarely ③ Sometimes ④ Often ⑤ Always

16. Do you deal constructively and logically with your problems?

① Never ② Rarely ③ Sometimes ④ Often ⑤ Always

17. Do you always try to think of your cup as half full instead of half empty?

① Never ② Rarely ③ Sometimes ④ Often ⑤ Always

18. Do you always do what makes you happy as long as it doesn't hurt anyone?

① Never ② Rarely ③ Sometimes ④ Often ⑤ Always

19. Do you always try to accentuate the positive and de-emphasize the negative?

① Never ② Rarely ③ Sometimes ④ Often ⑤ Always

20. Do you help others whenever possible?

① Never ② Rarely ③ Sometimes ④ Often ⑤ Always

21. Do you choose to forgive yourself and others?

① Never ② Rarely ③ Sometimes ④ Often ⑤ Always

22. Do you try to let go of negative past experiences?

① Never ② Rarely ③ Sometimes ④ Often ⑤ Always

23. If you find yourself thinking a mean or negative thought, do you correct yourself internally and rephrase it into a kind and positive thought?

① Never ② Rarely ③ Sometimes ④ Often ⑤ Always

24. Do you always remind yourself that you always get back what you put out (including a smile)?

① Never ② Rarely ③ Sometimes ④ Often ⑤ Always

25. Do you learn to like yourself by doing, thinking, and saying things that are authentic and pleasing to you?

① Never ② Rarely ③ Sometimes ④ Often ⑤ Always

26. Have you become the kind of person that you would love to have as a friend?

① Never ② Rarely ③ Sometimes ④ Often ⑤ Always

27. Do you live in harmony with your good values and morals?

① Never ② Rarely ③ Sometimes ④ Often ⑤ Always

28. Do you always strive to do what is right?

① Never ② Rarely ③ Sometimes ④ Often ⑤ Always

29. Do you practice daily truth and integrity of your thoughts, intentions, and actions?

① Never ② Rarely ③ Sometimes ④ Often ⑤ Always

30. Do you participate in a community that supports you?

① Never ② Rarely ③ Sometimes ④ Often ⑤ Always

31. Do you choose to focus on the good things about your life?

① Never ② Rarely ③ Sometimes ④ Often ⑤ Always

32. Do you do something proactively to change or shift what is wrong with your life and then move on?

① Never ② Rarely ③ Sometimes ④ Often ⑤ Always

33. How often do you take control of the reins of your life or depend on others to do it for you?

① Never ② Rarely ③ Sometimes ④ Often ⑤ Always

34. Are you in touch with a sense of purpose in your life?

① Never ② Rarely ③ Sometimes ④ Often ⑤ Always

35. Do you work professionally at something you enjoy?

① Never ② Rarely ③ Sometimes ④ Often ⑤ Always

36. Do you enjoy the "journey" of life and the "process" of achieving?

① Never ② Rarely ③ Sometimes ④ Often ⑤ Always

37. Do you reach out to make new, more positive friends and develop closer relationships?

① Never ② Rarely ③ Sometimes ④ Often ⑤ Always

38. Do you put out "positive vibes?"

① Never ② Rarely ③ Sometimes ④ Often ⑤ Always

39. Do you feel like you *belong* to the outside world?

① Never ② Rarely ③ Sometimes ④ Often ⑤ Always

40. Do you strive to be happy or always want to be right?

① Never ② Rarely ③ Sometimes ④ Often ⑤ Always

Calculate the Positive Currency in Your Happiness Bank

Add up the numbers next to your answers and find out how filled up your happiness bank is. Don't worry if it's not what you'd like, because there is always room to grow your account. Each day is a new day, a new investment opportunity.

181-200 **You are a Happiness Mogul**
You are very lucky and have undoubtedly worked hard to create the kind of sustainable happiness

that makes you a pretty joyful person most of the time. Of course, it would be great to be happy all of the time, but that's not realistic. Get busy making and doing wonderful things for others who aren't as blessed as you are.

161-180 **You are a Happiness Millionaire**

Being a millionaire is great, but why not reach for the happiness sky? Strive to nourish your life with even more emotionally uplifting influences, thoughts, and actions. So, if your score isn't quite perfect consider the times your *H-Factor* goes askew, and use your high Happiness IQ to bring it back in line in due course.

136-160 **Your Happiness Bank is Full**

While having a full happiness bank is great and may make you feel secure, there will always be those rough times when external events challenge your joy and you will have to dip into the stored reserves of your happiness investment account to help you keep perspective and bounce back when things are not perfect. Make sure that you always replenish what you take out through good self-care.

100-135 √ **Your Happiness Account is in the Red**

Your bank account is a little low on happiness and you need to find a way to generate more joy for peace and contentment. Whether it's planning new things to do that will make you happy, like traveling or joining a club, or whether it's getting rid of some of the toxic people in your life, try to bulk up your account with more positive thoughts and nurturing actions.

39 to 99 **Your Happiness Account is Overdrawn**

You are in deep happiness trouble, even in "happiness debt". This is when your sadness (liabilities) are greater than your happiness (assets) and you can't figure out a way to get out of this unhappy dilemma. Following the suggestions in this book will boost your happiness currency to yield a greater positive return on your investment. It is possible to rewire your inner-thoughts to reflect a more ideal and productive way of thinking and being in the world.

Through this book, you are going to get great information, user-friendly tools and simple proven interventions to help you raise your *H-Factor*. Perhaps you are feeling as though you are just fighting to stay emotionally afloat and the thought of change is a daunting proposition. Remember Rome was not built in a day and change happens through measured and persistent efforts. You can prove to yourself through trial and error that change for the better does occur when we invest a small amount of consistent effort. And when we receive a positive result, even if it's only one minute of relief, we feel good and see the possibility for more.

We then continue to establish new habits by reprogramming and practicing more uplifting supportive thoughts, intentions and actions and the minutes become hours and hours become days and days become weeks and weeks can become lasting transformation of our perspectives and our lives. Baby steps. Be kind, loving and accepting of yourself as you learn new ways of being in the world that are more positively and productively self-honoring.

"Happiness is when what you think and
what you do are in harmony."

~ *Mahatma Gandhi* ~

Key #1: Life is tough, but happiness is available to all

We all have a story to tell. Regardless of our personal histories, a good life really is available to all of us, no matter where we come from. It is essential that we understand that suffering is just a natural part of life. It need not define who we are or keep us from joy. But it does present us with a puzzle that we are required to solve.

> "Being happy doesn't mean everything is perfect. It means you've decided to look beyond the imperfections."
>
> *~ Unknown ~*

Many years ago there lived a woman whose life was not what it seemed. That woman was me—a reformed depressed person. I'm not just the expert offering advice that I haven't test-driven myself. I am a living and breathing example of someone who has fully embraced the practices of applied positive psychology, spiritual psychology, and mindfulness interventions to change my life.

Positive psychology is an applied approach to optimal functioning and sustainable well-being emphasizing a proactive approach to life. Practical interventions enhance human strengths and character virtues while focusing more positively on what's right with life rather than wallowing in what's wrong with it.

Spiritual psychology is an exploration of the numinous or divine, sacred, or holy parts of the human experience. This encompasses investigation of the spiritual dimension as the essence of the psychological inquiry and quest for self-actualization. Thus offering a conscious awakening of the authentic self and a letting go of what disturbs our peace.

Mindfulness is the practice of present awareness of our thoughts, feelings, emotions, bodies, and environments. Through mindfulness we become a nonjudgmental witness to our lives without believing in the "right" or "wrong" way of our experience. We observe, we feel and we allow what is with acceptance,

empathy, compassion, and loving-kindness. When we are mindful, we are showing up for life focused in the present moment. In the here and now there is no space for rumination about the past or the future.

I come from a normally dysfunctional, imperfectly perfect family that has many skeletons in its closet: depression, divorce, addiction, suicide, rape, mental illness, physical illness, significant loss, and loads of unfulfilled dreams.

As an adolescent, I recognized the signs of depression that were looming in my mind and began exploring them. My hope was to uncover and illuminate the veil of darkness within me. My heart and mind were so heavy and it was exhausting carrying around their weight. It was hard and I was unsuccessful more often than not, but I still longed for the change. I knew something had to be there. Finally, as an adult I did find the way—through education, practice, and commitment—to apply positive and spiritual psychology techniques along with mindfulness practices in service to my mental health. In addition, I became disciplined and consistently proactive in my lifestyle management including rigorous exercise, good nutrition, daily meditation, and at times, psychotherapy to support my integrated well-being. I discovered that I was the one who could change my world. It started with me. Such a daunting and liberating acknowledgement.

Recognizing that I was the only one who could set me free, initiated a series of events into motion that are my guiding force to the work I do today. I went back to college for a master's degree, I continued researching ways to manage depression, anxiety, lack of motivation, self-mastery, and heal trauma. And probably one of the most valuable things I discovered is that the most healing salve of all to soothe our suffering is the application of love, compassion, and kindness to ourselves. It has been said that healing is the application of love to the places that hurt. I help people discover and nourish their happiness. But there are none that I am more passionate about than those who are striving to recover from addiction, trauma, and life crises. I think of myself as an emotional triage specialist who supports people in transforming their uninvited and unwelcomed experiences into events of profound meaning and growth. This requires creating a tool kit of powerful coping skills—like the hoe to loosen the top soil so you can get to the rich stuff that's underneath, or it may be the water that helps nourish what's there so it can grow up toward the sun and become stronger with each passing day.

Reflecting back on my journey helps bring it all into perspective. Once upon a time I was a chic, savvy, yet unhappy-inside urban mom who set out to discover my "purpose" by enrolling in a graduate studies program in psychology, where I produced a documentary film entitled, *"H-Factor . . . Where is My Heart?"* as my final thesis project. My hope was to create a film that would show others what my life was like *before* I started to ask myself the hard questions —like what will I contribute to this world before I die, what are my gifts and how will I share them, what makes me a good, successful and joyful person, and what is the legacy I want to give my children—and how it transformed *after* I asked them and found some of the answers that I'm sharing with you in this book.

It wasn't easy.

I wanted to stay in the same familiar place I'd almost always been in. It wasn't great, but I was comfortable enough. I didn't want to "rock the boat" or do anything that might cause others to think I was having some sort of crisis. This type of thinking did not change the fact that something needed to change. I knew I wasn't happy. I knew it deep down. But what did I even know about how to attain true happiness?

In my previous life I was the stereotypical young trophy wife married to a much older man. In my former role, I was ensconced in a busy, bold, and chaotic life filled with two beautiful children, a seemingly loving husband (I say seemingly because sadly, our relationship later disintegrated due to misaligned values on many levels), a large network of friends and family, travel, fashion, jewelry, cars, and homes—I had every appearance of having it all. Yet none of it was enough. On the outside, I was living a "happy life," never lacking in things but internally, I lacked authentic, meaningful joy.

I was thirsting for change and determined to educate and grow myself to create a more peaceful, meaningful, and contented life. After so many years of building a warm, nurturing home, raising children, and cultivating a marriage, it had been a long time since I had dared to take the time to think about myself and my own happiness. I was parched from the years of focusing on everyone else.

I had a hunch that true and sustainable happiness would become available to me upon my realization of a greater sense of passion, purpose, place, and meaning in life. After all, that's what all the self-help gurus would always say: if you find your passion, you'll find your happiness. I believed it. So, at the tender age of forty-one, I went back to school to simultaneously complete the last year of my bachelor's degree in architectural design studies and the first year of my graduate degree in psychology.

Architecture and psychology have a lot more in common than most people recognize. And these two subjects were my passions. I wanted to make them blend together—as they do in systems like Feng Shui, a method of designing spaces that uplift and harmonize everyone within the structural environment.

Architecture is about designing physical space, and psychology is about organizing mental worlds. Still, while I might have been able to create a structure for a house, creating my own inner structure did not seem as easy as drawing up a blueprint. What I did know was that I was determined to figure out how to create a new, better life for myself. And in doing so, I became a more positive role model for the people in my life, especially my kids, who were deeply impacted by my return to school.

It was a daunting task to attempt two academic years at once. As a young college student straight out of high school, I probably would not have taken this on. But for me, at the threshold of mid-life, I realized I had nothing to lose and everything to gain. It was time to stop worrying so much about what I *couldn't* do. No longer would I just wander from one thing to the next, trying to find a way to satisfy my desire for "something." That doesn't mean I wasn't afraid from time to time; I was. But I also knew I was on the right track to creating a more authentic and fulfilling life for myself and a positive role model for my kids.

My initial goal was to complete my graduate studies and become a licensed clinical psychologist, seeing

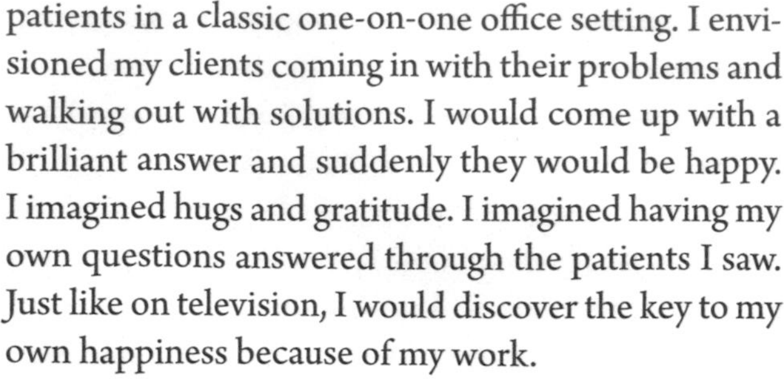

patients in a classic one-on-one office setting. I envisioned my clients coming in with their problems and walking out with solutions. I would come up with a brilliant answer and suddenly they would be happy. I imagined hugs and gratitude. I imagined having my own questions answered through the patients I saw. Just like on television, I would discover the key to my own happiness because of my work.

Soon after I began my master's program, I realized I did not believe I had the patience to sit within the confines of an office, day in and day out, hour after hour, listening to other people's problems; this conventional setting was not a good fit for me.

That was one of many wake-up calls. Another wake-up call was the realization that in real life, we usually don't solve our chronic issues quickly but bit by bit over time—like the normal growth process.

I was dedicating myself to a program when I already knew I couldn't follow through with it as a profession. Did that mean I had wasted all of my time and money on a silly dreams? Did this mean that happiness was even farther away than I'd thought it to be?

Was this just *another* example of how my big dreams were nothing more than illusions?

Of course not. It was all part of my journey and contributed enormously to my quest for greater happiness.

Ironically, many years later, a good part of my days are spent sitting with people in deep crisis, supporting them as they heal and change their lives.

Personal stories. We all have them, don't we? If you look around your local bookstore, you'll notice a recurring genre in the bestsellers—memoirs. Sharing our stories can be liberating, especially when they inspire others.

But our stories can become our prisons, too.

When we continue to tell ourselves that we are defined by a certain experience or that there is only a certain future story we can enjoy, we limit who we are.

Think about your last job and how that ended. If it ended badly, you probably were nervous about your next job, thinking about whether you were going to have the same experience in your new role. You may have replayed your old story in your head—over and over again—trying to better understand what went "wrong" and overcome your upset about it. But sometimes, just thinking about these stories and infusing them with a lot of emotional energy each time can cause them to repeat themselves.

"Our past is a story existing only in our minds.
Look, analyze, understand, and forgive.
Then, as quickly as possible, chuck it."

~ *Marianne Williamson* ~

What we forget sometimes—well, what we forget *often*—is that the stories that *have* happened to us are not the stories that *will* happen to us. As Rev. Michael Beckwith says, "Your history is not your destiny." The stories people tell us about how things *should be* or how things *have always been* are just that: stories. They are not facts. They are not guaranteed. They are merely options. History is not a rulebook nor is it destined to repeat itself.

Stories, whether they are our own or the stories of those around us, can inspire or destroy. When stories fail to teach something new, or if they just remind us of things we regret and cannot change, these stories hold us back.

Think about the stories you tell yourself. Indeed, you probably have many. You tell yourself these stories because you think they are important. But if they don't contribute to your happiness, it's time to do what Marianne Williamson says to do: *Look, analyze, understand, and forgive.* Then chuck them.

The stories you tell yourself must empower you not hold you back.

True happiness is born of experience not ignorance. Embrace the experiences you are dealt—even when they are negative. Sometimes, it is only after weathering a storm that we understand what true happiness really feels and looks like. Take what you can from the negative experiences and then let them go. Let them pass over you like a warm breeze on a summer night.

This unknown quote often attributed to Buddha puts it into perspective: "Pain is inevitable. Suffering is optional." These words are simple, and so true. We will all experience pain to some degree in our lives. This comes with living life whether we take a lot of chances or play it safe. However, needless suffering does not have to be a part of our destiny. Truly, it serves no purpose aside from stifling us from learning from a moment, accepting the reality of a situation (even one we do not like, such as the death of a loved one). It is our relationship to the suffering we inflict upon ourselves that predicts our life experience. Do we become defined by it? Will we choose to be unhappy or will we allow a transformation to take place? This choice is ours.

Let me revisit a scorching-hot day long ago while I was bicycling in northern India. That's right. Picture me as my former princess self, biking in the 110° heat in Rajasthan near the Pakistan border.

"Lucky" is the word that drifted in and out of my mind as I traveled the bumpy roads. I was far away from the comfort zone of my world—and intentionally so. This was my first chance in years to be away from my children and spouse. I was grateful for the opportunity to explore myself in an environment so different from the familiar. I was able to take a break from my old stories for a bit. By removing myself from the way things *were* in my life, I hoped to find out how they *could be* when I returned.

For a few years prior to my visit, my former husband and I had donated money to the Sulaxmi School for Girls in Lucknow, India, to support students who normally would not have access to even basic education. These were children of the streets, many of whom called a tarp strung between two trees "home" and had never been to school. The school's mission was and is to give these girls a fundamental education. Learning reading, writing, and arithmetic would enable them to later work and become independent. Although the education they received at the school was basic, it was far more than they had ever dreamed of achieving and it allowed them to earn money to help support their families and their villages. This small change in their lives could rescue girls from a life on the streets or the fate of an arranged childhood marriage. The school made me hopeful. By supporting it,

I knew I was doing something important for the girls I helped and for future generations. And through this I learned about the power of serving others in order to help change the world one act at a time. The surprise gift to me was greater happiness and deeper meaning in my life.

On this life-altering trip to India, I brought a small video camera with the intention of making a little promotional piece about the Sulaxmi School to raise money for it upon my return to the States. I wanted to capture the simplicity of its mission: to educate a generation of girls so the cycle of poverty could be broken. What I didn't realize at the time was that as I helped these girls, I also helped myself, ultimately changing the course of my life. I learned that I possessed the true power to contribute to transform myself and contribute to the change of others.

From this profound and heartfelt mission, I experienced firsthand a most powerful lesson: nothing is impossible. I proved to myself what Mahatma Gandhi wrote about the nature of personal and social transformation going hand in hand, "If we could change ourselves, the tendencies in the world would also change. As a man changes his own nature, so does the attitude of the world change towards him. . . . We need not wait to see what others do." I realized that I had the power to change my world and by changing my world I could touch the lives of others and inspire them to do the same.

Think about that for a moment. *Nothing is impossible.*

Although we tend to focus on what isn't possible in our lives, the truth is that we are powerful manifesting creatures. In the numerous villages I visited throughout India, where they lacked even basic essentials for life and growth, happiness existed and life was thriving. In these villages, I experienced joy that wasn't rooted in possessions.

I learned that one person can make a difference in the lives of many. And this was a lesson that resonated in my bones. I thought about how ripples in the water begin with the slightest touch on the water's surface. I thought about the way that I would be touching the lives of others halfway around the world through my video and with my voice.

By believing in myself, I could change the world around me. I could grow and stretch beyond my wildest expectations. Because I helped these girls, their expectations for themselves and for their futures grew. They were no longer limited by the stories they were born into and what they thought was going to happen to them. And neither was I.

As I rode through the Indian countryside, a bright-eyed, glaringly obvious Western tourist, I observed the beautiful nature of India's people—friendly, warm, inviting, and happy, despite the poverty surrounding them. What was the mysterious ingredient that allowed their joyful, inner light to radiate out through their eyes for all to see? I wanted to know.

My mission became and continues to be studying, educating, unlocking, and sharing these uncomplicated keys to a more joyful life.

Today, think about your personal story and the stories you tell yourself. Are they limited in definition and bound to a script authored perhaps in the past, out of date and irrelevant to the present? Ask yourself:

- What stories do you tell yourself again and again?

- What happens when you define yourself by and live solely within the stories you tell?
- What might happen if you decided to stop telling yourself old stories?
- What would happen if you rewrote your personal stories?
- Name ways in which past suffering has helped you in your present life (e.g., you're stronger, more resilient, more confident, less willing to take abuse from others).

Sustainable happiness exists regardless of scarcity or abundance, regardless of poverty or wealth, and regardless of external circumstance. Happiness is happening out there in the world, even if we are not happy. However, our personal happiness is available to us at any time because happiness is a choice and happiness is an inside job! Happiness is your inside job! That does not mean we are happy 100% of the time. It means we get to choose the stories we tell and how they impact our joy.

"The Work always leaves you with less of a story.
Who would you be without your story?
You never know until you inquire.
There is no story that is you or that leads to you.
Every story leads away from you.
Turn it around; undo it.
You are what exists before all stories.
You are what remains when the
story is understood."

~ Byron Katie ~

Being human means being a pleasure-seeking missile. We are hardwired for pleasure and desire to feel good. It's amazing. We also have an inherent distaste and aversion to discomfort, pain, and suffering. All living creatures do. We avoid those things at all costs, most likely. Yet, in our attempts to stay away from them, we become depressed, disconnected, isolated, addicted, and self-medicated with destructive drugs, behaviors, and even our own misery—the heart of the old adage that misery loves company.

How do we stop this discomfort in the face of those inevitable moments that don't meet our joyful expectations? The only way is to allow the difficult feelings to move through us. Our feelings are like the waves in the ocean. They ebb and flow. They come and they go. Happy people learn to surf on top of the waves rather allow themselves to be pulled into the barrel or sucked into the undertow of them. That is how we acknowledge, heal, and grow upward. When we resist, discomfort persistently pursues us, growing steam and strength that is stronger than the resistance we give. It's self destructive to the point where we must confront our limits of no longer being able to "live like this anymore". We retaliate by yelling, screaming, self-destructing (or worse) until we finally seek out and ask for help.

Living in the darkness of needless pain and suffering is not healthy, productive, or happy. It robs us of joy and well-being. Don't allow your misery to be the weeds that seep into your garden and wreak havoc. When we lean into our pain and confront the source of our sadness with love, empathy, and curiosity, our lives are transformed.

Bill's story

A few years back I worked with a Viet-Nam Veteran named Bill. He was a former sniper who was a raging alcoholic and could not figure out what motivated his self-destructive behavior. Finally, when he was on death's doorstep from alcohol poisoning, he acknowledged the guilt and shame he felt from having killed numerous innocent children, and cozying up with his male cohort and "spotter" to fill his empty heart with warmth and connection. He never shared these intimacies with his wife who he referred to as his best friend, lover, and soul mate of more than 50 years. Bill did not identify as gay but courageously recalled his heartsickness and profound moral injury. He sought comfort the only way he could given his circumstances. And yet, his trauma nearly took him down until he went to rehab, surrendered to a solid 12-step recovery program, got a sponsor, worked his steps, and began to practice being fully present, releasing judgments and savoring the goodness in his life. This was hard work for Bill and his sobriety was a hard-won prize after multiple relapses and continued self-compassion, mercy, and love.

"Without your wounds where would your
power be? The very angels themselves cannot
persuade the wretched and blundering children
on Earth as can one human being broken
on the wheels of living. In love's service,
only the wounded soldiers can serve."

~ *Thornton Wilder* ~

Identifying Your Happiness Quotient

It's time to test your HQ. Your HQ differs from your *H-Factor* and your Intelligence Quotient because it shows how you deal with life's ups and downs and how resilient you are in the face of setbacks and stress.

We all have unconscious thoughts and behaviors that sabotage our happiness. By analyzing our inner-thoughts and feelings, we can determine whether we currently have a high HQ and only need a happiness "tune-up" once in a while or whether we have a low HQ and our unhappiness is coming from self-inflicted wounds created by negative inner chatter. You can actually raise your HQ at any stage of life by learning how to reprogram your inner-thoughts. You'll find various techniques on how to do this throughout this book. You can even achieve relief from taking a few conscious breaths, accepting that you are right here, right now, and applying some effort to building a little more happiness into your life.

Mark the number that best describes your answer to each question:

1. Do you repress your true feelings?

⑤ Never ④ Rarely ③ Sometimes ② Often ① Always

2. Do you feel "controlled" and afraid to "let go"?

⑤ Never ④ Rarely ③ Sometimes ② Often ① Always

3. Do you usually have positive expectations?

① Never ② Rarely ③ Sometimes ④ Often ⑤ Always

4. Do you feel happy most of the time?

① Never ② Rarely ③ Sometimes ④ Often ⑤ Always

5. Do you look forward to waking up in the morning?

① Never ② Rarely ③ Sometimes ④ Often ⑤ Always

6. Do you feel "out of character" if you appear "too happy" to others?

⑤ Never ④ Rarely ③ Sometimes ② Often ① Always

7. Do you push unhappy emotions under the rug?

⑤ Never ④ Rarely ③ Sometimes ② Often ① Always

8. Do you discuss unhappy emotions with close friends and family?

① Never ② Rarely ③ Sometimes ④ Often ⑤ Always

9. Do you ever feel like a victim?

⑤ Never ④ Rarely ③ Sometimes ② Often ① Always

10. Do you feel like you are the master of your own destiny?

① Never ② Rarely ③ Sometimes ④ Often ⑤ Always

11. Do you have mean-spirited and negative judgments of yourself and others?

⑤ Never ④ Rarely ③ Sometimes ② Often ① Always

12. Is your inner-dialogue negative and cruel?

⑤ Never ④ Rarely ③ Sometimes ② Often ① Always

13. Do you exercise regularly?

① Never ② Rarely ③ Sometimes ④ Often ⑤ Always

14. Do you feel comfortable and healthy in your body?

① Never ② Rarely ③ Sometimes ④ Often ⑤ Always

15. How does your body respond to stressful situations?

⑤ Never ④ Rarely ③ Sometimes ② Often ① Always

16. Is illness a frequent visitor to your life?

⑤ Never ④ Rarely ③ Sometimes ② Often ① Always

17. Do you have satisfying and connected relationships?

① Never ② Rarely ③ Sometimes ④ Often ⑤ Always

18. Do you eat well-balanced meals?

① Never ② Rarely ③ Sometimes ④ Often ⑤ Always

19. Do you sleep between 6 – 8 hours per night?

① Never ② Rarely ③ Sometimes ④ Often ⑤ Always

20. Do you engage in hobbies you enjoy?

① Never ② Rarely ③ Sometimes ④ Often ⑤ Always

21. Do you engage in volunteer work you enjoy?

① Never ② Rarely ③ Sometimes ④ Often ⑤ Always

22. Do you have any addictions to substances and/or behaviors?

⑤ Never ④ Rarely ③ Sometimes ② Often ① Always

23. Do you try to turn negatives into positives by seeing the silver lining in situations?

① Never ② Rarely ③ Sometimes ④ Often ⑤ Always

24. Do you worry about things you have no control over?

⑤ Never ④ Rarely ③ Sometimes ② Often ① Always

25. Do you try to learn from every negative experience?

① Never ② Rarely ③ Sometimes ④ Often ⑤ Always

26. Do you have a goal in life that will benefit yourself and others?

① Never ② Rarely ③ Sometimes ④ Often ⑤ Always

27. Do you feel you have a purpose in life?

① Never ② Rarely ③ Sometimes ④ Often ⑤ Always

28. Do you compare your life to others?

⑤ Never ④ Rarely ③ Sometimes ② Often ① Always

29. Does it seem like others have a better life than you do?

⑤ Never ④ Rarely ③ Sometimes ② Often ① Always

30. Do you focus mostly on yourself and your problems?

⑤ Never ④ Rarely ③ Sometimes ② Often ① Always

31. Are you a good listener?

① Never ② Rarely ③ Sometimes ④ Often ⑤ Always

32. Do you ramble on about yourself and your problems to others?

⑤ Never ④ Rarely ③ Sometimes ② Often ① Always

33. Do you wallow in self-pity?

⑤ Never ④ Rarely ③ Sometimes ② Often ① Always

34. Do you feel insecure or threatened by people and events around you?

⑤ Never ④ Rarely ③ Sometimes ② Often ① Always

35. Do you sometimes secretly wish bad things would happen to some people you know?

⑤ Never ④ Rarely ③ Sometimes ② Often ① Always

36. Do you think there's enough abundance in the world for everyone?

① Never ② Rarely ③ Sometimes ④ Often ⑤ Always

37. Do too many problems sink you into depression and despair?

⑤ Never ④ Rarely ③ Sometimes ② Often ① Always

38. Are you always worrying about what others think?

⑤ Never ④ Rarely ③ Sometimes ② Often ① Always

39. Are you always beating yourself up for past mistakes?

⑤ Never ④ Rarely ③ Sometimes ② Often ① Always

40. Do you always dwell on what is wrong with your life?

⑤ Never ④ Rarely ③ Sometimes ② Often ① Always

41. Do you feel your life is out of control?

⑤ Never ④ Rarely ③ Sometimes ② Often ① Always

42. Are you stubborn?

⑤ Never ④ Rarely ③ Sometimes ② Often ① Always

43. Are you able to see other peoples' points of view?

⑤ Never ④ Rarely ③ Sometimes ② Often ① Always

44. Are you open to the idea of changing the way you see life?

① Never ② Rarely ③ Sometimes ④ Often ⑤ Always

Score your HQ

Add up the numbers next to your answers and find out how much you know about how to achieve authentic happiness—the genuine stuff that radiates from within you! If you aren't where you want to be, it's exciting to know that you can change that. And this book will help you do that.

186-220 Very High

If you have a very high HQ it means that you may be blessed with a "happy brain" and/or you have learned how to deal with life's ups and downs in a very positive way. Your life-coping skills are very high and you are very resilient to the forces that could sabotage your happiness if you let them. Work on maintaining, even increasing, your wonderful life skills as you age and help others do the same.

166-185 High

A high HQ means that your life is generally happy and the way you deal with everyday problems is excellent. Even people with very high HQ are not immune to unhappy moments. They may simply bounce back more rapidly for a variety of reasons. If and when you feel unhappy, it is usually due to a temporary lapse in life coping skills—perhaps because of stress, fatigue, hormones, or external circumstances beyond your control. Work on using your high HQ to talk yourself through these rough patches.

141-165 Average

If your HQ is average, work on raising it. Become more aware of your reactions to everyday problems and situations. Do your reactions make you unhappy? This, of course, involves analyzing how you interact with others and how you let external events affect your internal happiness. Use discernment and positive choices to increase your HQ.

106-140 Low

A low HQ is usually due to a lifetime of acting and reacting to life's ups and downs in unhelpful ways, mixed with some genetic unhappiness and dysfunctional early modeling. If your parents were negative and that's all you heard as you were growing up, your brain will be wired for a negativity bias. To some degree, all brains are because pessimism was an essential survival strategy for our ancient ancestors. The challenge will be for you to retrain your brain to process incoming information in a more positive way. Please know that there are many ways to retrain negative thought patterns, and you can learn them with the help of this book.

44-105 Very Low

If your HQ is very low, you are probably both genetically unhappy and have very low life-coping skills, perhaps due to how you were raised or current life circumstances that keep you from thinking and processing life events in a more positive and constructive way. It is very possible to raise your very low HQ by determining which ways of thinking and acting are sabotaging your happiness, and then reversing those behaviors one by one. Yes, this is a challenge, but it can be done!

"When I hear somebody sigh, 'Life is hard,'
I am always tempted to ask, 'Compared to what?'"

~ *Sydney J. Harris* ~

Key #2: Be your own guru

We become our own best guides by learning to listen to ourselves. Have a chat with your inner child. Our inner child is that wonderfully spontaneous little one who doesn't care what everyone else thinks and hasn't become jaded by the harsh realities of adult life—this is who we need! This little one knows exactly where our happiness is hidden.

"Life has no meaning.
Each of us has meaning and we bring it to life.
It is a waste to be asking the question
when you are the answer."

~ Joseph Campbell ~

Just for a moment, stop and think about your day. Did you laugh today (even if only for a moment)? Probably not as much as you used to. Statistics show that children laugh an average of 80% more per day than adults. That's because children view their world through a different lens than we do. They seek out and create joy for themselves naturally. Beyond that, children laugh unconditionally—they don't allow external or internal negativity to impact their appreciation of joyful moments when they arise. Children are naturally curious and filled with wonder about life.

Instead of worrying about everything that could possibly go wrong, most healthy, well-loved children believe that life is exciting and happy. Why do they think this way? Because they aren't weighed down by responsibilities and by the unhappy stories we adults frequently tell ourselves. Young children don't stop to think about the past. They don't have one. They simply do what brings them joy in the moment and are rewarded with happiness and laughter.

Have you noticed how children don't have filters? They'll just tell you what they think. And they have opinions about everything, including all the negative, difficult things we try our best to shield them from. The difference is their outlook: they are open, hopeful, curious, and optimistic. Children are whimsical

and authentic in their emotional expression. It is the stories we tell ourselves that oftentimes hide the joy that is always within us.

It comes down to spontaneity and responsibility. When we are young and carefree, we simply take each moment as it comes, enjoy it, and then seek out another to replace it. We don't go back and forth about how things *could* be better. Depending on our experiences and our role models, we develop positive or negative views of the world as being a hospitable or a scary place. As children we are highly impressionable and depending on the age of the child and whether their experiences are basically positive or negative at home and school will contribute to the global view of life. It also depends on what they see modeled in the media. Like I shared earlier, we are hard wired for pleasure and dislike discomfort. Sometimes resistance to fully experience and deal with what is really going on robs us of our happiness and perpetuates needless suffering. If we focus on the moment we are in and make the most of it—even if that means we fashion a toy out of a ball of string instead of having an expensive Barbie doll or toy car—we can find pleasure in our lives.

It isn't until we start school and board the "Achievement Express" to college that we begin to feel the weight of responsibility, expectations, and obligations. We become aware of—and oftentimes dwell on—our weaknesses. We may do things because we want to fit in instead of doing things to make ourselves happy. Children will do many self-forsaking things to gain their parents' love and social approval. As adults we often continue to do the same thing. We become less invested in the moment and more consumed with the future. Everyone starts to ask, *"What do you want to be when you grow up?"* and if we don't know, or if we have the *wrong* answer, we start to question our self-worth.

Oh, how quickly the carefree pleasures of childhood disappear!

In order to be "successful" adults, we think we need to be more resolute, more serious, and more somber. We can't "waste" our time playing, laughing, simply being happy. We have more important things to take care of. Our to-do lists keep growing longer, our need to impress others becomes all encompassing, and we settle for being what everyone else thinks we should be.

It's no wonder that we can't seem to be spontaneous anymore.

You've probably found yourself in the situation where someone has asked you to take a step off your perfectly constructed path, a step you hadn't anticipated taking. Maybe it's a matter of taking an impromptu trip to a new country or getting involved in a volunteer organization that would cut into your weekends. Even though you could have participated (and maybe even secretly desired to) in these unexpected opportunities, you didn't. The thought of a change in plans, disruption to your routine—especially one that would take you away from work—stressed you out, so you passed on it.

And then you regretted your decision. And then it was too late to do anything about it.

The truth is that we all have responsibilities. We will always have one more thing to cross off our to-do lists.

But that doesn't mean we can't take advantage of unexpected opportunities. Old-school thought told us to think happy thoughts and then we would be happier. New school thinking suggests that action follows emotion. Therefore, if we are not feeling happy or good, we should go out and do something that

will foster a shift in our thoughts and feelings. You've heard of the "fake it 'til you make it" method?

Where have all your smiles gone? Have you tucked them away for certain people or for certain occasions? Have you decided that smiling makes you look immature or somehow ignorant of the realities of your oh-so-serious life?

While happy times are certainly good times to smile, they are not the only times. When you release an unexpected smile, you are choosing to show up in the world in a more positive light demonstrating that happiness, caring, and joy are possible—at *any time*. You remind yourself that happiness is available even when times are hard and your life feels dark. Each one of us has an internal pilot light within and when we are feeling energetically low or mired in internal darkness, that flame has diminished and needs to be fanned with fresh air to increase that light source that helps to illuminate our path.

In truth, it's actually more important to laugh during difficult times than happy ones because laughter is a release. It breaks up tension. It helps you breathe. Think about a time when you were consoling a friend who lost a loved one. At first, you grieve with her. You cry. You comfort. But then, you make a joke and your friend laughs for the first time in days. And you laugh with her.

And didn't that feel great? Didn't the laughter help the situation as much or more than the tears?

Reporting on a study by Dr. Robin Dunbar and others, James Gorman wrote in *The New York Times*: "Laughter is regularly promoted as a source of health and well being, but it has been hard to pin down exactly why laughing until it hurts feels so good. The answer, reports Robin Dunbar, an evolutionary psychologist at Oxford, is not the intellectual pleasure of cerebral humor, but the physical act of laughing. The simple muscular exertions involved in producing the familiar ha, ha, ha, he said, trigger an increase in endorphins, the brain chemicals known for their feel-good effect."[1]

You only need to remember that your inner child is just as smart—if not smarter than—the adult version of you because it is the most authentic version of you. By tapping into your inner child, you create a connection between your true self and the self that you've been presenting to the world for the past ten, twenty, thirty or more years. The best part? Your inner child knows exactly where you've concealed your happiness.

Like any good investigator, ask your inner child some questions to see what your little one wants and needs to be happy. Don't worry if this is difficult at first. It's like reconnecting with an old friend: things may be a little awkward at first, but once you start talking, you'll instantly remember why you connected in the first place.

Start by asking your inner child:

- What makes you happy?
- Would having *more* (x, y, or z) make you happier?
- What do you want to try that you haven't tried before?
- What have you done in the past to be happy that might look a little silly as an adult? (Do it anyway!)

These are simple questions—questions you might have skipped over in the past because you thought you already knew the answers. But until you ask your inner child these questions, chances are you really won't be aware of your truth. When you ask your inner child, your answers won't be hindered or filtered by the stories you've told yourself or what society

considers the "right" answers. Because this isn't about what *should* make you happy: this is about finding out what actually does make you happy, *right now*. Here are some suggestions for reawakening and reacquainting yourself with your inner child:

- Coloring
- Singing
- Blowing bubbles
- Hopping and skipping
- Surround yourself with childhood photos
- Howling at the moon
- Make a collage
- Eat your favorite childhood food
- Write your little self a love letter

What happens to your mood when you engage in fun-loving spontaneous activities that are amusing and childlike? Does it make you feel good? Does it make you happy? Does it make you feel alive and present?

What makes you smile? What makes you excited? What makes you want to jump up and down with enthusiasm? What makes your heart sing? When we consult our inner child, we tap into our quiet inner wisdom that can guide us towards greater joy because we are aligned with our true character. People often think they're making up the answers and have a hard time trusting the wise messages that come through when they tune into themselves. But once you have your inner child's attention and give him or her the respect, kindness, honor, mercy, and love he or she deserves it becomes easier to calm the choir of critics that lives in your head. And when we can silence the undermining, nay-saying voices that tell us everything we cannot or should not or mustn't even dare to do, we can begin to trust ourselves.

Self-trust means knowing that we can take care of ourselves. We believe that we have what it takes to provide for our basic safety and needs. Self-trust means we muster the courage needed to survive and then thrive. The gift of self-trust is the commitment to the refusal to give up on ourselves in our quest to experience a meaningful life.

People and life may seem to betray us. People change their minds and life is ever changing. But that's not a reason to give up on love, connection, and the desire to belong. However, it is a reason to bolster the relationship we have with the one person we can always count on being there for us: ourself!

So stop contemplating what you think others may be thinking about you. Instead of seeking answers and validation externally, look within yourself because the journey to happiness isn't about everyone else. This journey is about *you.*

Many times we come to realize that the truth—or what we really knew was best—has existed within us the entire time at a deeper level of awareness. Maybe because of external pressure—or what we feared others might think of us—we chose to ignore it and to abandon our intuition instead of embracing it. By doing this, we were unknowingly supporting self-destructive and self-limiting storytelling that keeps us stuck in victim consciousness.

When we do follow our intuition, it's a very different outcome. We are able to tap into the innate wisdom of our inner child and can recognize the destructive nature of numbing our feelings.

We numb our willingness to feel what's really going on inside of us through distractions and addictions—to work, to intoxicating substances, to self-de-

structive behavior. All of these are forms of emotional numbing and there are hundreds of ways we do this. Some methods are more destructive than others but they all seek to produce the same result—temporarily ending the discomfort of our emotions. We surrender to our intolerance of what we are feeling because we are afraid we cannot handle the sadness, the grief, the loss, the pain, the fear, the shame, the guilt, or even the reality of our circumstance. Our greatest fear is that we cannot bear or contain what comes up if we really allow ourselves to feel.

There is a paradox here, which is that what we resist persists. By running away from our feelings we create tension and discord within ourselves. But what would happen if we agreed to muster a little courage and look directly at what lies beneath that numbing? By simply leaning into that discomfort (the yucky stuff we don't want to face) and trusting that we can handle all our emotions whether painful or pleasurable, we gain a sense of peace and freedom. We remember that every thought and feeling is temporary and passes just like the waves in the ocean, a rainstorm, or a gust of wind.

"We wait all these years to find someone
who understands us, I thought, someone
who accepts us as we are, someone with a
wizard's power to melt stone to sunlight, who
can bring us happiness in spite of trials, who
can face our dragons in the night, who can
transform us into the soul we choose to be.
Just yesterday I found that magical someone
is the face we see in the mirror: It's us and
[underneath] our homemade masks."

~ Richard Bach ~

Addicted to Numbing

> "Numbing the pain for a while will make it worse when you finally feel it."
>
> ~ *Professor Albus Dumbledore* ~

Think about the experience of our foot falling asleep and the pins and needles and aching we feel when it awakens. We sit on our foot for a while and temporarily compress the nerves in it and don't feel the discomfort until we move our foot. Suddenly our body becomes charged with energy and starts sending signals to our brain. The same holds true when we sit on our feelings. We become disconnected from what we think and feel and separated from our hearts. In that state we don't experience the negative aspects of that unwanted feeling until we start awakening it when we are willing to move by changing our perspective.

When people hear the word "addiction" they automatically focus on typical substances such as alcohol and drugs. However, running away from our "self," dis-

comfort, and "what is" is an equally addictive behavior. Truthfully, people can numb themselves in many ways besides getting involved with substance abuse. We numb ourselves through our work—becoming addicted to our laptops and cellphones. As philosopher, social worker, and researcher, Brené Brown PhD says, "We don't want to turn off our machines because what if we miss something? An email? A text? A FB post? A blog? What if?" Well, the world goes on. Our world continues. Far too many people have become addicted to their technology. It's a way of connecting but at a distance. It's a way of being with others but still being alone. It's a false sense of intimacy.

Other ways we numb ourselves:

- Distancing ourselves emotionally.
- Overeating.
- Gambling.
- Abusive relationships which are an unhealthy attachment to physically and/or emotionally violent partners with whom we cosign a very toxic codependency.
- Living an overly busy life; filling every moment with something.
- Obsessively watching television.
- Spending excessive time on the Internet.
- Rage-a-holism (growing intensely angered over even the smallest of things—such as the person who writes the check in the grocery store line instead of using their bank card).
- Workaholism.
- Shopping.
- Sex.
- Pornography.

- Somatic medical problems (nothing is wrong with us but we don't feel well, our bodies hurt, and we are constantly seeking a diagnosis of something, anything but the truth of our feelings and emotions).

The emotional numbing and other forms of addictive behavior we participate in causes a vicious cycle that begins with discomfort and discontent before circling to guilt and shame, and eventually fear of vulnerability and loss of control. Welcome to the merry-go-round of unhappiness—the ride that just keeps going until you decide to get off.

When we feel shame it makes us anxious. Not only because we experience fear, but also because it may lead us to believe and feel that we are out of control—like a runaway train. Add in some self-doubt (those feelings that we just aren't good enough) and we really grow numb because we see no other way to cope with what's happening to us. At least the numbness takes the edge off, right?

Of course, for some people the experience is very different. One friend told me that she endured "decades of 'psychic agony' that nothing could numb except my own creative work." The gift in that for her is that the pain pushed her to do a lot of healing inner work. And her focus on her creative gifts has enabled her to make a living through them.

Can you think of some ways you have begun to numb yourself recently or in the past? Why do we engage in numbing behavior? It's a strategy to help us avoid experiencing pain.

Numbing can also be intricately connected to trauma. When a person has been abused or trau-

matized they will often dissociate from the world around them in order not to feel the pain of the trauma/abuse. In order to heal from this pattern, we need to develop greater awareness often through expert counseling/therapy. With a professional you will begin to understand why you numb out, how you do so, and how to replace numbing behavior with healthy behaviors.

Here are a few simple, kind and loving self-soothing techniques that allow you to remain in your body and be present with whatever feelings are arising within you:

- Take a walk.
- Take a bath.
- Mindfulness practices (awareness of body, breath, senses, environment).
- Play beautiful music.
- Read uplifting material.
- Draw.
- Journal.
- Sing.
- Constructively whine for 5 minutes with a timer and then immediately move onto another activity.
- Ground yourself through breathing, visualization, or meditation.
- Zoom out the lens of your perspective. View the situation from 10 feet above you to reframe what you see (and feel). This is also known as gaining a meta-view.

Otherwise the feelings will surface in other ways. We can develop headaches, gain or lose weight, engage in dysfunctional relationships, develop chronic pain, sleep disorders, etc. It's vital to confront the pain we're trying to numb and face it head on with expert support.

We gain significant benefits by "defrosting" emotionally and accessing a deeper level of feelings. These benefits often include improved health on all levels, heightened intuition, improved relationships, more acute sensing, and a generally more happy and peaceful life.

"We all need to look into
the dark side of our nature—
that's where the energy is, the passion.
People are afraid of that because it holds
pieces of us we've been busy denying."

~ *Sue Grafton* ~

Polishing the reflection in the mirror

Observing and reflecting on how we respond emotionally and physically to various situations provides us with invaluable self-education. Educating ourselves is a part of the transformation we seek. If we are the garden, becoming wise to ourselves is the organic fertilizer that will help nurture us to grow stronger, wiser, more intuitive, and emotionally intelligent.

Check out the questionnaire below and mark down your answers to the questions. By so doing, you'll grow more aware of how you respond, and understand that you do have control. You will learn something valuable in your quest to stop using numbing as a form of coping.

1. I know why I engage in numbing behavior.
   ☑ Yes ○ No ○ Unsure

2. I am fully aware of which emotions I am trying to numb.
   ☑ Yes ○ No ○ Unsure

3. I have been unaware until now that I was engaging in numbing behavior.
   ○ Yes ☑ No ○ Unsure

4. I have been unaware of which emotions I was trying to numb.
   ○ Yes ☑ No ○ Unsure

5. I am fully aware of the triggers for my numbing behavior.
   ☑ Yes ○ No ○ Unsure

6. I am unsure as to what triggers my numbing behavior.
   ○ Yes ☑ No ○ Unsure

7. I use busy-ness as a way to numb my feelings.
   ○ Yes ☑ No ○ Unsure

8. I use alcohol as a way to numb my feelings.
   ☑ Yes ○ No ○ Unsure

9. I use drugs as a way to numb my feelings.
   ○ Yes ☑ No ○ Unsure

10. I find myself in dysfunctional relationships.
    ☑ Yes ○ No ○ Unsure

11. I avoid social situations as a way to protect my feelings.

  ○ Yes ✓No ○ Unsure

12. I use gambling as a way to numb my feelings.

  ○ Yes ✓No ○ Unsure

13. I use the Internet as a way to numb out to my feelings.

  ○ Yes ✓No ○ Unsure

14. I am ready to work on this to create a more positive, healthy lifestyle.

  ✓Yes ○ No ○ Unsure

15. I am not yet ready to work on this to create a more positive, healthy lifestyle.

  ○ Yes ✓No ○ Unsure

We are all addicted to something, even if it is the simple joys of chocolate, a favorite TV series, or something far more destructive that gets in the way of life. Remember, we are always striving for pleasure and desiring to minimize discomfort. Many of us use common numbing techniques in one of four varying degrees:

1. Experimentally
2. Recreationally
3. Abusively
4. Addictively

How, when, where, and why do you numb?

Becoming aware of where we struggle and how we put up our "emotional boxing gloves" against happi-

ness helps us to learn more about our addictive behaviors and how we freeze and block certain emotions within us so they can never escape.

This allows us to see where our own mind has kept us separated from our own possibilities for happiness in the present. We cannot fix the past but we can begin the healing process and gift ourselves permission to enjoy happiness today.

Neale Donald Walsch states it so simply:" Life begins at the end of your comfort zone."

Ursula's story

A young new mom came to me for coaching after recently being discharged from a psychiatric hospital. She arrived at my office with bandages on both wrists resulting from an attempted suicide. Ursula was an only child and during her mother's illness the daughter was the primary caregiver. Unbeknownst to Ursula, she became pregnant and did not know it until six months into her pregnancy. Her mother died and she gave birth within a few weeks to her son. My client was grieving and post-partum-ing simultaneously.

Her depression drove her to the precipice of self-demise. After months of her hard work, the sight, sound, feel, and taste of life returned to her. During our last session she stated that she would not kill herself because she is "just too damn curious about what comes next. Ursula committed to not abandon her baby or leave him with a legacy of trauma. Thankfully she sought treatment by a team that could provide her with comprehensive psychiatric, psychological, and lifestyle management support.

A perpetual winter inside of us is a stifling thought, but we can avoid it from becoming our reality. If you're really ready and committed to liberating from self-limiting patterns and beliefs then put yourself into situations that you know in advance are likely to bring up uncomfortable feelings. In other words, step outside your comfort zone. Find some triggers that can help you see and acknowledge what you may be avoiding due to discomfort, fear, and pain. Whenever you acknowledge one of these things, take a moment to breathe in and find a way to connect with something that will help you recognize what you are experiencing, accept it to the best of your present ability, and then guide yourself to a happier thought, even if that thought is, "This too shall pass."

A wonderful way to gracefully melt these frozen feelings is to give ourselves opportunities for a deep thaw. Sometimes we need to obtain the support of skilled experts to help us better cope with our lives. This step requires honesty and courage. Asking for assistance is a compassionate act of self love. I call this out-sourcing support by calling in experts to help just as you would call a plumber for a clogged sink or toilet. And when we are good to ourselves and do so, we grow stronger and happier.

"Surviving is important, thriving is elegant."

~ *Maya Angelou* ~

Engage in self-compassion

Compassion for others is wonderful and an essential quality in life. All too often, however, we neglect ourselves in the process. We're so busy being good to others that we forget to attend to ourselves. Self-compassion is one of the ways we can let go of these numbing behaviors, in combination with other tools, of course.

Here are some ways to begin:

a. Write yourself a self-kindness memo daily for the next two weeks. Each day write a note to yourself in kind, gentle tones and remind yourself of how wonderful you are. Say specific things like: "Congratulations. You did a great job at . . . " or "It was so nice of you to reach out to . . . " Really mean it when you write it and feel it when you read it!
b. Try writing yourself a letter from a "future you." In this letter you have overcome these numbing behaviors. Explain how you did it. Congratulate yourself for being successful with the journey.
c. Create a vision board, which is a visual reminder of what you wish to see transform in your life. You can write a story, paint a picture, or take photographs that emanate something about self-compassion to help remind you. Add inspiring words or quotes that anchor in your mind the area of change you desire. Put this up in a place where you'll frequently see it, read from it out loud, and stay in touch with your many reminders about why you want and need self-compassion.
d. Take breaks! If you can afford it, take a physical break—a spa day or a mini-vacation. Go somewhere wonderful, even if it's just for a day. Or, get some friends together and go for a walk or to the museum. Set up a potluck. Organize a birthday celebration for a friend. Do fun things

that break the negative pattern. Find a group of happy people to socialize with.

Both sadness and happiness are contagious. People who are sad tend to isolate themselves and become socially disconnected. But those who are happy—you guessed it—surround themselves with other joyful, connected, and emotionally healthy people. While not all of us are hardwired for joy, we can all develop the techniques to take us to a more joyful place. It's our choice and how we direct our focus is what catalyzes the shift. Why not give yourself permission to experience joy rather than just simply avoid pain?

"The attempt to escape from pain
is what creates more pain."

~ *Gabor Maté* ~

Are You Hardwired for Joy?

"Happiness is when what you think,
what you say and what you do are in harmony."

~ Mahatma Gandhi ~

This section is going to help you answer an important question—*Are you hardwired for joy*? There are those of us who are genetically depressed, and it takes effort to balance what we have been given that's less favorable than a happier state of being. We must grow and nurture joy, never taking it for granted and feeding off the abundance of good feelings that it gives us.

In this chapter, you'll become more aware of how to identify symptoms you may be having that should really be treated by a psychologist, therapist, or psychiatrist. You'll also learn more about how you can begin a journey to authentic happiness. At any time, you can choose to create a happier life.

Dr. Sonja Lyubomirsky, author of *The How of Happiness*, coauthored a paper with Matthew D. Della Porta titled "Boosting Happiness and Buttressing Resilience." In it they discussed how 60% of our tendency toward joy is nature and 40% is nurture. According to the paper, "A person's chronic happiness is determined by three factors: 1) a genetically determined happiness 'set-point,' 2) happiness-relevant circumstantial factors and 3) happiness-relevant activities and practices." Our families are not only our blood, they are a part of our DNA. We may not be able to eliminate what we've been given biologically. However, we do have ways to overcome a more depressed state so we can focus on the joy that life will offer us if we create it. Creating joy involves engaging in activities that generate positive emotion and an increased sense of well-being. We may not always be able to change our external circumstance but we can change our relationship with what is going on around us.

Yes, it takes more effort for a depressed person to be happy than it takes a genetically happy person—but it can be done with courage, determination and tiny baby steps. And life is filled with sudden unhappy events that alter the course of a person's life in an instant.

Recovering from or bouncing back after trauma and hardship is not easy and the internal fortitude required to do so must never be minimized. However, just as one would train for a marathon, prepare a complicated food recipe, or decide to lose weight and become fit, our success is progressive. The ability to achieve goals that stretch the limits of our present comfort zone is what can also make them so inspiring and gratifying to accomplish. Yes, the process will produce some stress and uncertainty. However, I'm talking about the good kind, the kind of stress that

challenges us to go beyond perceived limitation to achieve a desired and valuable prize whose by-product is happiness. Happiness is not the goal; happiness is the elevated emotion that is the gift of the process. Happiness has a funny habit of sneaking up on us when we are not looking for it.

Think about your family and what exists within it in terms of mental health history, past and present. You should see clues as to why you may not be as happy as you think you should be. Discovering this and admitting it as an obstacle is a major step toward achieving happiness. By recognizing traumatic events, and family dynamics as well as emotional and behavioral patterns such as depression and addiction helps shed light on what might have contributed to your unhappiness. Talking about it with a therapist, counselor, clergy member, supportive friend, or family member or peer support group can be instrumental in the healing process. Doing so validates and normalizes the experience, de-stigmatizes the situation and allows us to know we are not alone, that we can allow ourselves the precious vulnerability that allows us to be seen, heard, and understood in spite of our discomfort. This process rebuilds trust in humanity and within ourselves.

"The most beautiful people we have known are
those who have known defeat, known suffering,
known struggle, known loss, and have found their
way out of the depths.
These persons have an appreciation, a sensitivity,
and an understanding of life that fills them with
compassion, gentleness, and
a deep loving concern.
Beautiful people do not just happen."

~ Dr. Elisabeth Kübler-Ross ~

Key #3: More is not always better

Sometimes less really is a whole lot more. Often we fail to realize that more is not better—it's just more! Opt for experience over objects. Focus on enjoying your journey, not attaining more stuff.

> "Abundance is a process of letting go;
> that which is empty can receive."
>
> ~ *Bryant H. McGill* ~

The quest for more. The thing that controls all of our lives.

What's interesting is that we think that the people who have just a few more perks than we do—a better job, a higher salary, a bigger house—are the ones who never have to worry about anything.

It can seem to us that they have it all.

But of course, oftentimes they don't. I like to call this the "theory of more" because when it comes to the very human quest for "more," things aren't always what they appear to be. So when we see people who have more than we have, we wonder why they aren't happier. We wonder why they're not smiling from ear to ear. If you've noticed this track in the theory that "more" is better, you're already aware that things aren't always what they appear to be.

More money, more fame, more power, more time, more stuff, more sex, more food, more wine, more Xanax, more sleep, more vacation, more friends, more connections—none of it will do the trick. You can have it all and still be unhappy.

Then there is the newest thing that we focus attention upon in the spirit of wanting "more". Think of social media: we want more likes, more friends, more comments, and more of everything else. Many people easily become obsessed with this, but does it ever fill us up internally? Do we find true joy from these pursuits?

Think of this as a bowl of water with a hole in it. No matter how many times you try to fill it up, the hole still leaks, and the bowl never gets filled. Though you may try to fill it again and again, something is preventing you from the fullness that you seek.

Deep down, you already know this. You know that having more isn't a solution. If it were, there would be a point at which you would have enough, and you would just be happy, right?

But having enough and just being happy isn't what we are taught. From an early age, we're taught that happiness depends on owning more stuff—from children's toys, like dolls and toy cars, to adult toys, like expensive shoes and sports cars. But who benefits from this way of living: us or the sellers of so-called happiness packaged in the form of consumer goods?

When you look at the items you own, the places you've been, the relationships you've developed, and the experiences you've had, what sticks out as being the most important and valuable part of your life? Is it the things you own?

Probably not. And yet, we spend a lot of time and energy focused on attaining and achieving things.

The concept and the illusion of "more" can be likened to a carrot at the end of a stick. No matter how fast you run, that carrot will always be out of reach. You will do everything you can, forgetting about everything else, because you want that one "carrot," even though it becomes clear you will never have it.

You will never reach the ideal amount of "more" because there *isn't* an ideal amount. Sure, the stores and the advertisements might try to make you believe that if you buy the one item they are pushing—the carrot they dangle in front of you—your life will be complete, and you will be happy. But of course, that's not true. Whatever product they're pushing is just the "gateway drug." You'll never actually get the sense of satisfaction you secretly hope the "carrot" can provide. Mass marketing has one primary purpose—to sell widgets designed to appear as something essential to your happiness.

What if you began to focus less on getting that thing you think you want, need, or desire, and more on the journey? What if you began to think about how to make your life's journey more fun? More relaxing? More inspired? More connected and more present? What if you begin to walk instead of run and started to look inside and around you instead of at that object of desire? In time, you might realize that although someone or something will always be dangling a shiny object in front of you, it doesn't have to be the only destination of your journey.

By focusing on your journey instead, you might even stop reaching for stuff entirely and realize how much you already have. And when you do, an amazing feeling will creep up all around you. (Hint: it's your happiness.) While you were focusing on your journey instead of the thing, your happiness developed naturally along the way.

Let me break this down a bit further. Most of us would agree that all we want is a happy life but what that means and how we get there is an individual pursuit based on some pretty well-known qualifiers. Most importantly, happiness is defined by the experience of a greater amount of positive effect than negative ones. The cornerstone of positive psychology is the cultivation of greater well-being as its goal. But how do we really define happiness and where does it actually come from?

Some researchers (Carr, 2004; Selim, 2008; Diener, Oishi & Lucas, 2003) define happiness as a by-product of several environmental factors such as income, job, health, family, relationships, moral values, etc. However, in the pursuit of understanding and obtaining happiness there appear to be two theoretical perspectives that most influence what makes people feel happy. These are the hedonic and eudaimonic approaches to happiness (Keyes, Shmotkin & Ryff, 2002).

Hedonic well-being is based upon our experience of increased pleasure and decreased pain in our daily lives. This is how we rate our internal emotional experience of what is going on around us. Hedonism is about engaging in self-pleasure, self-gratification and self-indulgence. Hedonic well-being is subjective and defined by how we perceive our mood and general life satisfaction (Carruthers & Hood, 2004) to include:

- Presence of positive mood
- Absence of negative mood
- Satisfaction in various life domains (work, home, partnership)
- Global life satisfaction

Eudaimonic well-being takes into account ideas of self-actualization, self-determination, high-functioning, and subjective well-being with happiness as the result of experiencing life purpose, challenges, and growth (Keyes et al., 2002; Deci & Ryan, 2000) and include:

- Sense of autonomy
- Purpose and meaning
- Self-expression
- Connection
- Social service
- Competence
- Personal growth
- Self-acceptance

Positive psychology encompasses both views in which happiness is defined in terms of a good, pleasant, and meaningful life (Norrish & Vella-Brodrick, 2008). Dr. Christopher Peterson et al., identified three pathways to happiness that could constitute authentic and stable happiness:

- Pleasure in enjoyable and positive life experiences that maximizes feeling good, elevates positive emotion and minimize negative emotion and discomfort.
- Engagement by being immersed and absorbed in the task at hand. I call this showing up for life and all that it requires and demands. Thus, happiness or the good life results from investment of self into all that we do resulting in growth, competence, and satisfaction that brings about happiness.
- Meaning is the process of having a sense of higher or noble purpose in life that is outside of self. A good and happy life results from using our character strengths and personal qualities to serve the greater good, hence creating a deeper appreciation for life.

The synergy that results from combining the expression of hedonic and eudaimonic well-being is

said to produce the most stable model of happiness (Vella-Brodrick, Park & Peterson, 2009; Carruthers & Hood, 2004).

Since 2010 I've hosted Harvesting Happiness Talk Radio, a global Internet podcast show receiving millions of downloads each year. During each episode I interview outstanding contemporary thought-leaders and change-agents who share their gifts, talents, and wisdom in contributing to making the world a better place in which to live. Our mission is to support and inspire our listeners to create a thriving life through greater passion, purpose, place, and meaning. My own personal definition of happiness or bliss is the experience of intoxication from life itself.

Let's get back to looking at the other side of more: less. When did less become such a horrible thing? And what are we comparing it to? Less than what? Perhaps we've linked "less" to things that are supposed to be important to us:

- Less time
- Less money
- Less happiness

But when we think about "more", we can see how "more" is causing just as much anxiety as "less" ever could.

- With less time, we have more worries. With more responsibilities, we have less time.
- With more money, we may have less time and often less happiness.
- With less happiness, we spend more money and have less time because we need to work more to pay for the things that were supposed to make us happier.

All of these things create endless cycles of scarcity, not having, and FOMO (fear of missing out).

Getting dizzy yet? The truth is that everything is interconnected in some way, and how we decide to act is oftentimes driven entirely by our perspective. If we think that having "more" will lead to happiness, we will pursue "more" regardless of the problems "more" brings into our lives—which is dangerous, because "more" is an illusory state of being. The concept of having more money and stuff is an illusion. Money cannot buy authentic and sustainable happiness. Money can buy comfort and physical security but it cannot purchase the kind of lasting happiness earlier described that comes from pleasure, purpose, and meaning.

When you have more things, you have more things to take care of. When you have more people in your life, you need to maintain more relationships. When you have more responsibilities, more things can go wrong.

So stop for a minute and think about your life with less.

What might happen if you had fewer responsibilities at home or at work? What might you do with that free time? Would you take up a new hobby? Sign up for a class? What would you do with this *space*?

If you had fewer things in your home, would you feel more open? Would you feel less cluttered and chaotic? What would you do with this *space*?

Suddenly, a world of opportunity opens up.

Here's what gets lost when you are consumed by your quest for "more": when there are already so many things cluttering your life, you reach a point where you can't make space for anything else. While

life might have an unlimited capacity to accept and to give new things, you do not. You can't take on more work than can fit into twenty-four hours. You can't buy more things than what fits in your home. And when that happens, there's no room for the things you truly need to be happy. Instead, you're engulfed by the stuff you thought you wanted.

Maybe more isn't such a great idea.

It's no wonder that the minimalist approach is becoming popular—trendy, even. People are seeking ways to simplify their lives and to learn to live with less. And what do they find?

Those who have less in their lives actually have more:

- Financial security: they're not paying for the upkeep of a lot of things. They're not paying for a larger house or a storage facility to hold their possessions.
- Time to do more meaningful and enjoyable things: they're not spending their time shopping or working too hard in order to maintain a certain lifestyle.
- Satisfaction: instead of focusing on that one idealized object of satisfaction that is always out of reach, minimalists are able to focus on what's important—what they already have.

This isn't to say you should run out right now and divest yourself of all worldly possessions, but this is a great time to think about what you do have. Put some thought into this, evaluating your physical possessions and your relationships, alike.

Now take a step back and think about the way you have been living. Are you living a meaningful, happy existence in this very moment? Or have you been focusing on the prizes you hope to accumulate in the future, giving up days and weeks and months of potential happiness along the way? By opting for experience over objects as the basis of our happiness, we begin to engage in life more presently, fully and joyfully.

Just checking in . . . Are you starting to see the potential for greater happiness in your life? *"A little,"* you say. *"But I have real problems in my life. I have real issues. Things that make it very hard to be happy!"*

Don't worry; we're going to tackle that, too. Happiness is a complicated matter, after all. You have problems, and I have problems too. And we can still be happy. Sometimes it just takes a bit of conscious awareness—acknowledging moments of inner attunement and what I like to call, divine "inner-vention."

"It was not the feeling of completeness
I so needed, but the feeling of not being empty."

~ Jonathan Safran Foer ~

Divinity for Skeptics and Seekers

"If a man is to live, he must be all alive, body, soul, mind, heart, spirit."

~ *Thomas Merton* ~

Divinity is all about the "inner-vention." By "inner-vention" I mean the sacred haven where we meet up with our Higher Self, Source, or Power that meets us with awe and helps us keep our egos in check. Scientific and spiritual communities both recognize that there are some mysteries that cannot be defined by a mathematical equation but follow some kind of unexplained order within the universe. We are not just speaking about traditional "religion" here, although it is a part of this for many individuals. Spirituality has common threads throughout all religious traditions with benefits that include:

- Strong social support from others with similar viewpoints.
- The ability to socialize with those we feel at harmony with.

- Opportunities for community service.
- Chances to make new friendships within a like-minded community.
- Feeling connected to something greater than one's self.
- Experiencing a sense of awe, mystery, wonder, and divinity through devotion.

When it comes to meditation as a form of spirituality, you'll find a connection to your well-being because of its stress relieving and calming effects. This helps to elevate positive thinking, as we are nourishing our roots and allowing our minds to grow in the sunshine, instead of lingering in the clouds. In 2012, H.G. Koenig conducted a study about spirituality and happiness, noting "of more than 326 peer-reviewed studies of mainly adult populations found that out of those 326 studies, 256 (79%) found only significant positive associations between religiosity/spirituality and well-being. The author postulated that the positive influence of religion or spirituality on well-being can be explained through a few key mechanisms, such as religion's role as a coping strategy and as a support system for pro-social behaviors. In addition, religious beliefs can potentially alter the way individuals cognitively react to stressors, and often, the precepts of most faiths decrease the likelihood of individuals experiencing particularly stressful life events (such as divorce or incarceration)." [1]

These findings are an interesting starting point to elevate our understanding of how being a naysayer about divinity can be a great disservice. The true spiritual challenge is creating a numinous practice

in everyday life by being a good person regardless of believing in God or religion. By numinous I mean a connection to the awe, wonder, mystery, and divine nature of life itself. When we recognize and appreciate the magic that lives within our precious and limited days we come to know a powerful form of spiritual practice.

Swiss psychiatrist Dr. Carl Jung wrote about the value of spiritual practice in service to healing our invisible wounds and how the process itself can be experienced as "divine inner-vention,"

"The main interest of my work is not concerned with the treatment of neuroses but rather with the approach to the numinous. But the fact that the approach to the numinous is the real therapy, and inasmuch as you attain to the numinous experience you are released from the curse of pathology. Even the very disease takes on a numinous character."

~ *Carl Jung* ~

Embracing a conscious mental, physical, and spiritual process in our healing is what helps us to become whole and return home to ourselves, comfortable in our own skin. Brené Brown PhD is an American scholar and researcher who has written extensively on shame, worthiness, courage, and vulnerability. In her books *Daring Greatly, The Gifts of Imperfection* and *Rising Strong* she writes about what she calls *"whole-hearted living"*. She challenges us to risk the rejection and hurt that we fear most and that has driven us to disconnect, isolate, and become depressed by mustering the courage to dive deeply into our personal healing process in order to get our needs met.

"A deep sense of love and belonging is an irreducible need of all people. We are biologically, cognitively, physically, and spiritually wired to love, to be loved, and to belong. When those needs are not met, we don't function as we were meant to. We break. We fall apart. We numb. We ache. We hurt others. We get sick."

~ *Brené Brown* ~

Here are some meaty and mindful questions to mull over:

1. What does the word "divine" mean to you?
2. What have you been taught since childhood about the notion of the divine?
3. What does the notion of "sacred space" mean to you?
4. What does the notion of "making life sacred" mean to you?
5. What kinds of sacred experiences would you like to have?
6. What do you hear when someone says the word "holy"? Or "holiness"? And what happens when we change the word to "whole" or "wholiness"? The notions of divine and holy have been battered a great deal in recent years. The likely reason is that their definitions have become high-

> ly distorted and the essence of sacredness has been diluted by dogma, abuse of power by clergy members, and nonsecular politics. Some people don't even want to hear the words anymore. However, I'm a proponent for reclaiming and redefining spiritual practice as a sense of "the modern divine". Our lives are hectic and complicated enough, but when we don't have a sense of faith or some form of serenity in our lives they become even more challenging.

When was the last time you contemplated the notions of divinity and holiness? For some people this means God and religion, that's all. Yet, as with so many concepts we can expand them by developing a much fuller and broader definition of what divinity means in a deeply personal way. By expanding our relationship to that which we find is sacred and divine, we can experience and enjoy deeper connection in our everyday lives.

For many of us the notion of "divine" is beginning to change. Instead of the traditional, historical ideas about spiritual practice, we're embracing new ones. When we allow a much broader interpretation of this notion of the divine that encompasses exploration, contemplation, and experience of the numinous presence in our day-to-day lives, it empowers us to take responsibility for defining and practicing the divine and divinity, holy and wholly in our own personal way that invites deeper connection and meaning to our journeys.

New ideas about the Divine and Divinity

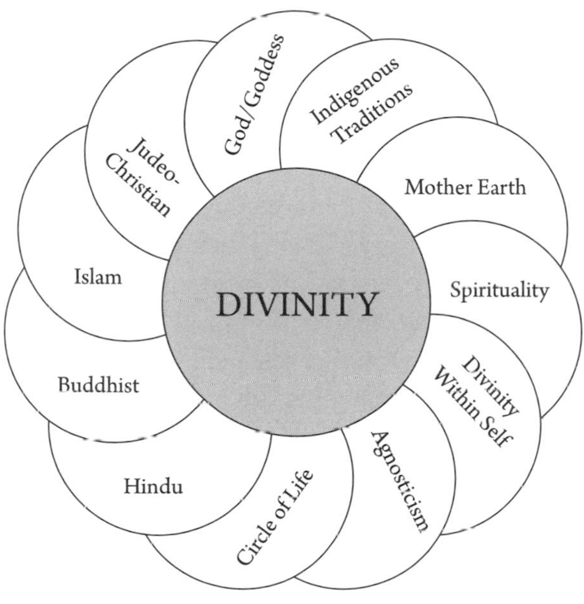

"Are you looking for me?
I am in the next seat.
My shoulder is against yours.
you will not find me in the stupas,
not in Indian shrine rooms,
nor in synagogues, nor in cathedrals:
not in masses, nor kirtans,
not in legs winding around your own neck,
nor in eating nothing but vegetables.
When you really look for me,
you will see me instantly —
you will find me in the tiniest house of time.
Kabir says: Student, tell me, what is God?
He is the breath inside the breath."

~ Kabir ~

One who is numinously inspired has a strong spiritual connection, which guides them in their decisions and actions as well as reactions. It provides a source of comfort and tranquility that helps someone deal with what is challenging, and awareness of what to be grateful for—even the smallest of things. This individual also knows that life's undesirable events do not have to take hold of them, as they are less fearful of addressing them and allowing their emotions to flow so they can learn, adapt, and move on in due course.

The most unexpected things can happen to us at unplanned times. These events are unscheduled and uninvited. In an instant they can be perceived as blessings or curses. But in some way, these challenges offer opportunities for "divine inner-ventions" that are meant to guide, teach, and transform us. As a result, life often places us on a happier track than the one we were on before. Some call this making lemonade out of lemons or seeing the silver lining. We simply need to pay attention and grasp the life lessons we can from it because we cannot change what has happened. In order to access that inner wisdom, we must quiet ourselves within ourselves to better listen to and lean into life. By doing so, we can then seek solutions and solace from within. And when we successfully access our inner counsel, we learn to trust ourselves.

Here's a personal favorite divine "inner-vention": Several years ago I was having a yard sale at the home that we were just about to lose as a result of my ex-husband's bankruptcy. A man and his wife pulled up and started buying some of our furnishings. We immediately had a lovely connection and spoke about our lives in general terms. They shared that they were opening a residential drug and alcohol addiction treatment center nearby. As we continued talking, they asked me about my profession and when I shared what I did they said they needed someone with my skills and hired me on the spot. Indeed, this was a powerful divine "inner-vention" because not only did I need work to support my family but it set me on the meaningful professional path upon which I travel to this day in supporting people in crises to heal and transform their traumas. Additionally this also was extremely fortunate for me as my ex-husband had recently stopped paying child support and the kids and I were headed for a deeply difficult financial road ahead. This event positively impacted and changed the course my life on every level because I was open to the opportunity, was paying attention, and proactively working to minimize the fear and uncertainty in my life at that moment.

Now, here are some big ideas to support your incorporation of the divine or holy into your life.

Finding meaning beyond yourself

If you already have a place where you go for spiritual nourishment, the best way to fully practice your spirituality is to get to know the people. Here are some questions to think about:

a. If you haven't been involved up until now why is that? Why are you holding back?
b. If you have been involved and it hasn't been fulfilling why is that so? Are you doing things by rote and not allowing yourself to have an emotional commitment?
c. What is your level of commitment to your spiritual life? Is it what you want it to be? If not, why is that so?

d. What is it you have to give or want to give to your community?

Do some spiritual shopping

Perhaps you've begun to evaluate or reconsider what you believe in and how you want to practice, it's time to do your spiritual shopping. So, what does this mean exactly? Well, it's exactly as it sounds—shop around! Start looking for spiritual communities and gathering centers in your city/town or nearby where you feel you would be comfortable. Now, this may not be an easy process, but it can be a lot of fun and certainly an adventure. Take your time, explore different places, attend spaces of spiritual practices, or go to other places that you feel may allow you to fully feel the experiences. Get a sense of who goes there. Do you feel comfortable? Have people welcomed you? How do you feel about the services; do you connect with them? Do they resonate inside of you? These are important questions to ask, along with how much it costs to be a member, and what kinds of commitments they ask members to make.

Consider exploring:

- Churches
- Synagogues
- Mosques
- Temples
- Atheist Groups
- Garden clubs
- Book clubs
- Cooking clubs
- Meet-ups
- Choirs
- Glee clubs

- Meditation circles
- Group therapy
- 12-Step meetings
- Support groups
- Hiking clubs
- Yoga
- Nonspecific spiritual study groups

Or try any other club or group that will help you generate more joy through connections with individuals with whom you share a kindred heart and common interests. If you are housebound or live in a remote location, many of the above choices offer virtual meetings by phone, chat room, and even live video sessions.

Investigating possibilities with curiosity

In order to have a deeper and more meaningful spiritual life, and bring a sense of the divine into your every day experience, you have to be willing to explore possibilities. But, if you don't explore the possibilities then you won't find them. Spirituality is something we uncover through exploration and discovery. It can take time to find a spiritual path, practice, and community that deeply resonates with our own values and principles. Here is an exercise to help you identify what might resonate best for you:

○ I seek a place where I can explore my spirituality

○ I seek a place where I can practice an open-minded form of spirituality

○ I seek a place where no single form of spirituality is practiced

○ I seek a place where the idea of God is all-embracing

- I seek a place where men and women can participate on equal terms
- I strongly identify myself as practicing a specific form of spiritual practice
- I believe in ideas such as reincarnation
- I don't wish to be affiliated with any notion of organized religion
- I want to engage in some form of spiritual meditation on a regular basis
- I already engage in a form of spiritual practice on a regular basis
- I like the idea of rewriting traditional prayers and transforming them into something more meaningful
- My spiritual practices influence my values, principles, and belief system
- I never identify myself as practicing one religion or another
- I identify myself as spiritual but not religious

"Stay close to anything that makes you glad you are alive."

~ *Hāfez* ~

Allow time to develop sacred rituals in your life

Ritual participation is one of the most beautiful things we can do for ourselves and in our lives. They help connect us to other people, the universe, and bring the divine/holy into our space. Here are ideas for rituals in the home:

- Rituals you create for yourself, such as: bathing, cooking, folding laundry, gardening, singing, making art, creative writing, etc. can be transformed into mindful practices that resonate with a spiritually connected feeling of being present, harmonious, and in what Hungarian psychologist Mihaly Csikszentmihalyi calls "flow" state.
- Celebrate summer or winter solstice by honoring the passing season and ushering in the new one.
- Holiday parties.
- Turn off all the lights and spend a moment in darkness, remembering and honoring the sun's light.
- Join a chorus, choir, or glee club.
- Gather around a campfire (or backyard fire pit) and sing, chant, share stories or poetry, say prayers.
- Organize a drumming circle.
- Create a sacred meditation space or inspirational altar with candles, photos, and talismans that offer you a sense of connection to your divinity.
- Organize a community circle that meets at regular intervals for singing, dancing, drumming, storytelling, prayer, etc.
- Pick flowers and make floral bouquets then distribute them to friends, neighbors, and colleagues.
- Bake and break bread with friends. There is something so nourishing about communing in fellowship with people we care about over a good meal.
- Organize a meditation circle or group.
- Design and make papier-mâché masks or vision boards with friends or your family.
- Honor Mother Earth—the Planet—by designing and creating your own ritual like planting or weeding a garden, cleaning up your local park, or learning how to compost.

Divine "Inner-ventions"

Remember how I shared my cycling experiences in India and what it brought forth? There I was riding my bike in physically challenging circumstances, but I was able to look beyond them and outside of myself to see something much bigger. That was a powerful divine "inner-vention" that led me to a path of self-inquiry, discovery, and transformation.

This experience took me into a place of understanding that I'd been seeking out, and now finally understood. I felt it. This feeling of witnessing your own "aha" moment is what this next set of questions is all about. Dive into your life's experiences and see what kind wonderful introspective life-altering moments or messages you can extract. The seeds of your divine "inner-ventions" are within you. It's time to sow them!

Have you ever had a divine "inner-vention"? More than once? Please write about them.

AFFECTION

How did each divine "inner-vention" change the course of your life?

____

____

____

____

____

What did you learn from each divine "inner-vention"?

____

____

____

____

____

Do you think that recognizing the divine "inner-ventions" in your life adds to your happiness?

✓ Yes

In what way?

____

____

____

____

____

O No

Why not?

____

____

____

____

____

____

Create a "Belief Manifesto"

This is a wonderful exercise and really allows you to stretch your creative muscles. A "Belief Manifesto" can help identify a vision that connects yourself with yourself on a soulful level. It's about finding the values and principles you hold most dear. Since this is about the divine this exercise will be limited to that domain.

I believe that the world was created by God.

O Yes O No

I believe that the world was created by a universal force but not necessarily the God we read about in the Old and New Testaments.

O Yes O No

I believe that the world was created in a purely random physical way known as the Big Bang.

O Yes O No

I don't believe there is a God in the universe.

O Yes O No

I believe in a Higher Power but don't necessarily know what that is.

○ Yes ✓ No

I don't believe there's such a thing as a God or a Higher Power in the universe.

○ Yes ✓ No

I believe that prayer or other form of spiritual meditation can be a beneficial part of one's life.

✓ Yes ○ No

I believe that prayer or other forms of spiritual meditation is completely unimportant and basically useless.

○ Yes ✓ No

I pray more fervently during difficult times.

✓ Yes ○ No

I rarely or never pray at all.

✓ Yes ○ No

I am interested in spirituality and the divine.

○ Yes ✓ No

I have no interest whatsoever in learning more about spirituality and the divine.

✓ Yes ○ No

I feel I have enough spirituality in my life.

○ Yes ✓ No

I could definitely use more spirituality in my life.

✓ Yes ○ No

If I were looking for a life partner I wouldn't care at all about their spiritual belief system.

○ Yes ✓ No

I would rather meditate than pray.

○ Yes ✓ No

I would like to combine meditation and prayer in my life.

✓ Yes ○ No

I believe people could use more spirituality in their lives in general.

✓ Yes ○ No

I believe connecting with the divine and holy elements in the universe are beneficial to me.

○ Yes ✓ No

I want to increase my connection to the divine and holy elements in the universe.

○ Yes ✓ No

I believe that connecting with divine and holy elements can help me find meaning.

○ Yes ✓ No

"Listen to the Music of the soul
With the chords of your heart attuned
With the strings of your thoughts in unison
With the Divine Musician"

~ Swami Jyotir Maya Nanda ~

Commit time to contribute to something you believe in

Many of my addiction and behavioral health coaching clients find the traditional and widely recommended 12-Step Group support path uncomfortable or not a good fit for their belief systems. Some are particularly challenged by the concepts powerlessness and surrendering their condition over to a Higher Power or God. I believe there is a way for anyone to connect with their wholeness or holiness, depending on your perspective.

Over the years I became acquainted with the profound writing of Noah Levine, an American Buddhist author and addiction recovery counselor who has written several books, among them *Refuge Recovery: A Buddhist Path to Recovering from Addiction.*

While I am not personally in addiction recovery, substance abuse has rocked my family on several occasions. I have come to know first hand the power of these programs to emotionally and socially support the healing process whether you are an addict, a loved one, or in need of some psychological structure in your life.

There is a huge need for something beyond traditional 12-Step recovery programs. One size does not fit all when seeking solutions to what ails the human heart and spirit. I see the tremendous value in peer-based support groups in the addiction and trauma recovery community I serve. I began researching alternatives and discovered Refuge Recovery based upon Buddhist teachings encompassing the desire to end needless suffering. In fact, I was so taken with the process and spirit of Refuge Recovery I established

a weekly group in my community as an alternative for those challenged by typical 12-Step dogma of surrendering to God or a Higher Power. This has been a huge source of joy in my life. I get to serve for the simple pleasure of being able to help others. These meetings continually elevate my mood and keep me grounded. Being of use to others from the heart and altruistically, especially when my own life might not be running 100% as smoothly as I'd like it to be, is one of the most powerful, best, cost-free, and natural anti-depressants I know.

The meetings have a simple format that involves brief and nonspecific introductions (one does not identify as an alcoholic or addict or disorder), a meditation, and a discussion based on Buddhist teachings and Refuge Recovery text. Participants are encouraged to speak about the benefits present in their lives resulting from the practice and encouraged to refrain from staying stuck in past stories. The community has welcomed this program with great enthusiasm as it is kind, compassionate, and absent of dogma of any kind. Refuge Recovery and all Buddhist teaching is based on the Four Noble Truths:

1. If we are alive, we will experience pain
2. The origin of our continued suffering is our attachment and desire for it to be different
3. It is possible to end our suffering
4. The way to end needless suffering is to follow the Eightfold Path

Traditional texts use the term "right" before each of the Eight-Fold Pathways. I have added my own perspective by changing this to "well-focused" to imply that our energy is harnessed and used wisely in service to our achievement. Here it is in a nutshell:

1. Well-focused view
2. Well-focused intention
3. Well-focused speech
4. Well-focused action
5. Well-focused livelihood
6. Well-focused effort
7. Well-focused mindfulness
8. Well-focused concentration

There are many ways you can engage in noble service within your community. This is another creative adventure you can take in order to integrate or increase the divine, holy, or wholly elements into your life. There is no shortage of issues to become involved with today. In fact, it's almost overwhelming how much need there is in our own communities, let alone the larger world. Here is a way to begin identifying the causes you might want to work with in order to integrate the spiritual or divine/holy elements into your life. When we give to others selflessly then we are truly giving to the world and raising our awareness that we are an interconnected part of a greater whole. As individuals, we are a part of the universe, not the center of it.

- Serve as a foster parent.
- Be a big brother or sister.
- Volunteer in a library, hospital, school, or community center.
- Serve on a committee or in another role in your spiritual community.
- Volunteer in a soup kitchen or homeless shelter.

- Volunteer in a shelter for abused women/children.
- Volunteer to be on the board of an established social service or agency. Every town has a community website or office offering opportunities for varying levels of involvement.
- Organize a group or committee in your neighborhood to keep it safe or clean it up (or both).
- Work or volunteer with an environmental group.
- Serve with an anti-poverty group.
- Organize a community lunch in your neighborhood.
- Organize a nature walk for the kids in your neighborhood.
- Volunteer in a seniors residence or nursing home.
- Become a baby-holder at a nearby hospital NICU.
- Open up your home for fundraising efforts.
- Offer to read for people who are blind (established agencies who work with people who are blind often have volunteer readers).
- Become a visitor for people who are in a hospice.
- Help someone you know who has had recent surgery or an illness.
- If you're a good cook, organize free cooking classes.
- If you like to knit or crochet, make blankets and sweaters and donate them.
- Collect jackets and blankets for agencies who distribute to people in need during the fall and winter.

> "You are here in order to enable the world
> to live more amply, with greater vision,
> with a finer spirit of hope and achievement.
> You are here to enrich the world."
>
> ~ *Woodrow Wilson* ~

Embark upon a quest for meaning

Spend time on a journey to find greater passion, purpose, place, and meaning in your life. Some of the techniques being used by many people today are:

- Meditation.
- Chanting or singing.
- Yoga.
- Contemplative walking.
- Energy healing practices such as Reiki.
- Creating your own mantras or affirmations (Ex. "I am a reflection of the light or I am connected and attuned to my Higher Power").
- Exploring mysticism.
- Charting family history and genealogy.
- Psychic healings and readings.
- Practicing the art of Zen.

A spiritual journey can be many things. Some people feel it's a time to get away from everything and everyone. There are people who leave their jobs and go travelling (something not recommended for everyone). They choose to backpack for a time and travel to distant places and spend time in new cultures. Some people want to spend extended times in nature. For some people, it might mean a walk in a park once a

day. A spiritual journey doesn't have to imply leaving home or your job. It can be exploring meditation at home on your sofa. It can be taking your camera out on a hike at a great park. Maybe there's a ravine you like to sit in and contemplate your life? These can all be spiritual journeys. The key is to find your spiritual desires and then take your journey.

Inspiration for the Spiritually Weary

For some of us the concept of spirituality is just not happening. Call it atheism, free-thinking, heathen or lapsed former ______________ (fill in the blank). There is no "there there" or buy-in with spirit. Consider the work of Don Miguel Ruiz, former surgeon, Mexican author and shaman in his most famous book, *The Four Agreements* originally published in 1997. In it he advocates shedding outmoded and self-limiting beliefs as well as prior nonproductive agreements we have made with ourselves and society that undermine our lives. Here are Ruiz's Four Agreements:

"1. Be Impeccable With Your Word

Speak with integrity. Say only what you mean. Avoid using the word to speak against yourself or to gossip about others. Use the power of your word in the direction of truth and love.

2. Don't Take Anything Personally

Nothing others do is because of you. What others say and do is a projection of their own reality, their own dream. When you are immune to the opinions and actions of others, you won't be the victim of needless suffering.

3. **Don't Make Assumptions** 

   Find the courage to ask questions and to express what you really want. Communicate with others as clearly as you can to avoid misunderstandings, sadness, and drama. With just this one agreement, you can completely transform your life.

4. **Always Do Your Best**

   Your best is going to change from moment to moment; it will be different when you are healthy as opposed to sick. Under any circumstance, simply do your best, and you will avoid self-judgment, self-abuse, and regret."

I am a long-time practitioner and advocate of The Four Agreements. Daily, I experience the positive impact and emotional liberation of keeping these Agreements and witness the success of my clients who also maintain them in their lives.

"The divine is not something high above us.
It is in heaven, it is in earth, it is inside us."

~ *Morihei Ueshiba* ~

Going Global with Gratitude

"Gratitude, the ability to count your blessings, is the ultimate way to connect with the heart."

~ Baptist de Pape ~

As we become more aware of the sacred and divine living within us, it becomes more natural to begin feeling more grateful for the simple pleasures and good things we do have in our lives. Even the smallest things such as an unexpected smile from a child we might pass in the grocery store can become a really wonderful moment that helps generate more positive emotion within us that will radiate outwards to others.

This is why gratitude and appreciation for our gifts both given and received is a positive practice that can spread goodness on a global level. I think we can all agree that gratitude is a positive state and happiness is a positive emotion. We also know that emotions are contagious, both the positive and negative ones.

When we are in gratitude we are emitting appreciation and upliftment, which has a domino effect.

Each of us has 86,400 seconds of daily once in a lifetime opportunity to be thankful. Every second is precious and unique. It doesn't seem so when there are so many of them so we take them for granted. Therefore I'm a big advocate of intentional gratitude by devoting a little time and energy to expressing thanks for the goodness in our lives. For some, this is a spiritual practice. And we only get one shot at that precise moment in time. Why not make them grateful?

Gratus is the Latin root word for gratitude; meaning appreciativeness, thankfulness, and gratefulness. Gratitude is positive acknowledgment for what we receive; albeit tangible or intangible. *Being gracious with our thankfulness is one way to validate the goodness in our lives.* It is a profoundly simple process that allows us perspective in recognizing the source of a blessing is oftentimes derived through another person, place, thing, or activity. Another positive attribute of gratitude is that it enables us to temporarily set aside our egos and connect to something greater than ourselves as individuals. This form of greater positive engagement with the world generates joy and reaffirms life.

Being grateful for each day and the good things in life is not something that should be reserved for once a year Thanksgiving traditions such as turkey and football.

Adopting an "attitude of gratitude" is a simple practice that can improve our health and create greater happiness in our lives.

In my years of practice as an applied positive psychology coach, I am continually amazed at the magnificent power that two of the most basic (and magic)

words, "thank you," can have on the giver and receiver of gratitude. Positive psychology research continuously supports this observation by reporting that gratitude helps harvest greater happiness.

Gratitude helps us build positive emotion, savor goodness, improves our well-being, cultivate meaningful relationships, and helps us to be more resilient at times when life is not a happy experience.

Dr. Robert Emmons, PhD, is one of the world's foremost scientific authorities on gratitude. Emmons theorizes that gratitude is the "queen of virtues" and wrote, *Thanks! How the Science of Gratitude Can Make You Happier.* In it, he states that by creating and maintaining a ritual practice of gratitude, we can increase our happiness levels by 25%.

What's so spectacular about gratitude? Gratitude is not simply a stand-alone virtue but one that is a call to action. Gratitude can be prescribed as a perfect antidote to rampant self-absorption and narcissistic entitlement prevalent in our complicated modern world.

When we are thankful, we are promoting an action that creates a positive reaction. Think of consistent thankfulness as creating a positive domino effect or spreading an infectious contagion of joy.

"Gratitude is born of humility, for it acknowledges the giftedness of the creation and the benevolence of the Creator. This recognition gives birth to acts marked by attention and responsibility. Ingratitude, on the other hand, is marked by hubris, which denies the gift, and this always leads to inattention, irresponsibility, and abuse."

~ *Mark T. Mitchell* ~

The key to cultivating meaningful, mood-altering gratitude is not in the mindless repetition of daily platitudes of "please and thank you". Rather, the art of being thankful is a "practice makes permanent" ritual expressed through conscious choice and focused attention on the heart.

Rituals, routines, and habits are subtly different invisible structures that help us organize our lives. In cultivating gratitude it is helpful to understand and focus in on the difference between the three processes:

- **Rituals** are a mindful process that commemorate an event and are designed to bring people together to become more focused on interconnection. Think of birthday parties and Thanksgiving meals.
- **Routines** are predictable activities that are consistently done the same way providing structure to the day such as preparing breakfast in the morning or going to the gym.
- **Habits** are unconscious repeated behaviors that become almost involuntary such as brushing your teeth or looking both ways before crossing the street.

Cultivating a solid gratitude practice, one that sticks, requires attention to all three of the above-mentioned methods:

- Creating rituals that celebrate and honor ourselves and others.
- Establishing routines that support paying attention to what is positively right with life.
- Adopting habits that encourage memory and acknowledgment of kindness, gifts, benefits, and goodness.

At the root of all of these practices is memory. An attitude of gratitude is all about remembering, in good times and in hard times. It has been said that our gratitude deficit comes from being collectively forgetful. We have forgotten to appreciate the rights and freedom we are afforded. We have forgotten to acknowledge those who have sacrificed on our behalf to preserve what we feel we are entitled to. We forget to express heartfelt thanks for the material advantages and things we think will make us happy.

Grateful people recall positive memories and emotions of being recipients of unexpected goodness, gifts, and grace, which they recognize and celebrate daily.

There are infinite ways to be thankfully grateful. And these practices are applicable for most ages and personal/professional environments. Why not make this a community project and enjoy the shift that will happen in your world?

"Let the beauty we love be what we do.
There are hundreds of ways to
kneel and kiss the ground."

~ *Rumi* ~

In his book, *Thanks! How the New Science of Gratitude Can Make You Happier,* researcher Robert Emmons wrote: "In gratitude and humility we turn to realities outside of ourselves. We become aware of our limitations and our need to rely on others. In gratitude and humility, we acknowledge the myth of self-sufficiency. We look upward and outward to the sources that sustain us. Becoming aware of realities greater than ourselves shields us from the illusion of being self-made, being here on this planet by right—expecting everything and owing nothing. The humble person says that life is a gift to be grateful for, not a right to be claimed. Humility ushers in a grateful response to life."

Harvesting your own gratitude practice requires awareness and the relentless practice of thank you, thank you, thank you! Focusing attention on your intentional appreciation is the first step in landing in a more thankful and emotionally uplifted state.

Here are a few suggestions to inspire your own creativity and expression of gratitude:

- **Gratitude Jar**: get a big old-fashioned mason jar and some index cards. Commit to writing three things for which you are grateful each day. Read them aloud each week to a friend, colleague, or family member to help anchor your appreciation.
- **Audio Gratitude**: record daily voice memos as gratitude memories and reminders that can be shared as emails or texts.
- **Video Gratitude**: create a daily short "selfie" video or "vine" of your gratitude and send them to those you appreciate.
- **Altar of Thanks**: dedicate an area in your home or office such as a shelf or fireplace mantle and add mementoes that remind you of your gratitude.
- **Inventory what you take for granted**: take a few minutes to write down some of the things you take for granted such as your magnificent body, the roof over your head, a hot shower, and the telephone. Imagine life without some of these blessings. Then imagine how you would

celebrate and honor these things if you lost them and then they returned to you.

- **Wall of Gratitude**: purchase some clothespins, string, and index cards. Stretch the string across a prominent place in your home or office. Write your daily gratitude on the index cards and pin them up on the line. Encourage family and friends to do the same on your wall. It's important to read your gratitude aloud as it helps concretize the appreciation for goodness stuff and helps ground us in the present moment of positive emotion.
- **Hot Seat of Thanks**: at a gathering designate one chair as the "Hot Seat of Thanks" where everyone gets a turn to sit and be the object of everyone else's gratitude.
- **Going Postal with Gratitude**: purchase or make 7 postcards and on them express your gratitude to the people in your life that matter and why. Send one a day for a week.
- **Text-festing Your Thanks**: create a group text to your friends, family, or colleagues offering gratitude for their gifts and presence in your life and watch it go viral.
- **Reframing the Bad Stuff**: recall events that seemed negative and unpleasant when they occurred and then reframe them and thank them for the learning opportunities they provided.
- **Pay It Forward**: this literally means taking a good deed someone has done for you and then doing a good deed for someone else. However, there are positive ways of doing this and of course the negative approach. When someone does something wonderful for us out of the

goodness of their heart they are doing a "mitzvah," an old Yiddish word for blessing or good deed. The key here is intent. If the intent is simply to help another person because we want to, then it's a good deed. But, if we do it because we are seeking reward or recognition or someone cajoled or embarrassed us into doing it then it's not really a pure good deed. Altruism is the virtue at work here.

Intent is extremely important in the concept of paying it forward. Here are 50 ideas to pay it forward:

1. Pay it Backward: buy coffee for the person behind you in line.
2. Compliment the first three people you talk to today.
3. Send a positive text message to five different people right now.
4. Post inspirational sticky notes around your neighborhood, office, school, etc.
5. Tell someone they dropped a dollar (even though they didn't). Then give them a dollar.
6. Donate old towels or blankets to an animal shelter.
7. Say "hi" to the person next to you on the elevator.
8. Surprise a neighbor with freshly baked cookies or treats!
9. Let someone go in front of you in line who only has a few items.
10. Leave a pre-paid gift card tucked at a gas pump or at the sink in a public restroom.
11. Throw a party to celebrate someone just for being who they are, which is awesome.
12. Have a LinkedIn account? Write a recommendation for a coworker or connection.
13. Leave quarters at the laundromat.

14. Encounter someone in customer service who is especially kind? Take an extra five minutes to tell their manager.
15. Leave unused coupons next to corresponding products in the grocery store.
16. Leave a note on someone's car telling them how awesome they parked.
17. Try to make sure every person in a group conversation feels included.
18. Write a kind message on your mirror with a dry erase marker for yourself, your significant other, or a family member.
19. Place positive body image notes in jean pockets at a department store.
20. Smile at five strangers.
21. Set an alarm on your phone to go off at three different times during the day. In those moments, breathe in, focus on your heart, then do something kind for someone else.
22. Send a gratitude email to a coworker who deserves more recognition.
23. Practice self-kindness and spend 30 minutes doing something you love today.
24. Give away stuff for free on Craig's List.
25. Write a gratitude list in the morning and again in the evening.
26. Know parents who could use a night out? Offer to babysit for free.
27. Hold up positive signs for people stuck in traffic or in a park for people exercising outside.
28. Return shopping carts for people at the grocery store.
29. Buy a plant. Put it in a terracotta pot. Write positive words that describe a friend on the pot. Give it to that friend.

30. Write a positive comment on your favorite blog, website, or a friend's social media account.
31. Have a cleanup party at a beach or park.
32. While you're out, compliment a parent on how well behaved their child is.
33. Leave a kind server the biggest tip you can afford.
34. When you're throwing something away on the street, pick up any litter around you and put that in the trash too.
35. Pay the toll for the person behind you.
36. Put 50 paper hearts in a box. On each cutout write something that is special about your partner or a friend. Give them the box and tell them to pull out a heart any time they need a pick-me-up.
37. Everyone is important. Learn the names of your office security guard, the person at the front desk, and other people you see every day. Greet them by name. Also say "hello" to strangers and smile. These acts of kindness are so easy, and they almost always make people smile.
38. Write your partner a list of things you love about him or her.
39. Purchase extra dog or cat food and bring it to an animal shelter or give it to a homeless dog owner.
40. Give a homeless person your doggie-bag or buy an extra sandwich to share.
41. Take flowers or treats to the nurses' station at your nearest hospital.
42. Keep an extra umbrella at work so you can lend it out when it rains.
43. Send a thank you card or note to the officers at your local police or fire station.
44. Take muffins or cookies to your local librarians.
45. Run an errand for a family member who is busy.

46. Leave a box of goodies in your mailbox for your mail carrier.
47. Tape coins around a playground for kids to find.
48. Put your phone away while in the company of others.
49. Email or write to a former teacher who made a difference in your life.
50. When you hear that discouraging voice in your head, counter it by telling yourself something positive—you deserve kindness and appreciation, too!

"Act in earnest and you will become earnest in all you do."

~ *William James* ~

Gratitude is one of the most beautiful ways we have of connecting to the divine and sacred. When we practice being grateful, the focus is on the positive rather than the negative. It's all too easy in our daily lives to become overwhelmed by our challenges. When we turn the focus around 180°, we're focusing on the good in our lives. The easiest way to practice gratitude is to begin practicing on a daily basis.

Even in the most difficult of times there can be things to be grateful for. But research is showing that practicing gratitude may be good for our health.

This is from the Greater Good Science Center at the University of Berkeley:

"Recently scientists have begun to chart a course of research aimed at understanding gratitude and the circumstances in which it flourishes or diminishes.

They're finding that people who practice gratitude consistently report a host of benefits:

- Stronger immune systems and lower blood pressure;
- Higher levels of positive emotions;
- More joy, optimism, and happiness;
- Acting with more generosity and compassion;
- Feeling less lonely and isolated."[2]

Psychologist Dr. Richard Grieger suggests that it's all in the power of our focus: "The focus of our mind matters. Why? Because we tend to act to produce that which we focus on. That explains the power of goals. By focusing on a desired goal, we tend, all things being equal, to act to make that goal a reality. To the contrary, by focusing on all the obstacles that make it hard to accomplish a goal, we discourage ourselves from acting to make that goal a reality."[3]

The same is true for our mood. Try focusing on everything negative in your life for one day and see what happens to your mood. Then, the next day, focus on nothing but the positive in your life, and watch your mood elevate. In my private practice I coach my clients to focus their attention in the direction of their desired destination and to enjoy the journey. Zig Ziglar, the famed motivational author, speaker, and consummate salesman wrote, " You hit what you aim at."

"You gotta look for the good in the bad,
the happy in your sad,
the gain in your pain and what makes
you grateful not hateful."

~ *Karen Salmansohn* ~

Investing in Ourselves

"A hunch is creativity trying to tell you something.

~ Frank Capra ~

How often have you heard someone, or yourself say things like this?

1. I had a funny feeling.
2. I should've listened to my instincts.
3. Why didn't I trust myself?
4. I knew this wasn't right for me, why did I do it anyway?
5. When am I going to learn that I know what's right for me?

At some time or another we all distrust ourselves. Perhaps we've been taught to do so. We might have been raised with a great deal of fear and paranoia. Or, perhaps we had a seminal experience early on in life that caused us to become distrustful of our own judgment. In truth, we will make mistakes. It's almost impossible not to unless we're the Buddha. The ability to trust ourselves, to be guided by our own instincts and respect our inner knowing is a muscle we must strengthen. As with other aspects of our personal growth, we learn and grow stronger over time. Let's begin by defining what we mean by intuition, exactly:

> Instinct and Intuition, as *I define them,* are as follows:
>
> **Instinct** is our innate inclination toward a particular behavior (as opposed to a learned response). A gut feeling—or a hunch—is a sensation that appears quickly in consciousness (noticeable enough to be acted on if one chooses to) without us being fully aware of the underlying reasons for its occurrence.
>
> **Intuition** is a process that gives us the ability to know something directly without analytic reasoning, bridging the gap between the conscious and unconscious parts of our mind, and also between instinct and reason.
>
> Here's another way of looking at it:
>
> Intuition operates in the realm between the conscious and the unconscious—amorphous and ethereal. Because intuition stems from the subconscious, from deep within our brain, it appears before us only to vanish—like a column of smoke—when we try to grasp it. We most often find it difficult to justify our intuitions rationally or say where they came from.

Today, the reality is we live in a world dominated by science and technology. We have this compulsive-like need and desire for information and it is easy to seek out. It's everywhere! Wanting facts and infor-

mation is a human instinct. We'll even pay to receive if we believe it'll be of great value. We can download things in an instant, and this feels gratifying, yes, but we must ask: is it also fulfilling? Does it make us feel better about ourselves, our world, and the joy and happiness that we can extract from it?

Making good decisions involves more than reason. The facts don't always tell the entire story. Haven't you ever been in a situation where you had a "gut response" to someone? You can't always tell why but it's there nevertheless. Even though the facts may say this is an upstanding person, there may be things going on underneath. For example, when Richard Nixon was President of the United States, at first people thought it was unthinkable that he had anything to do with Watergate. As the facts spilled out through the ongoing investigation however, Nixon's involvement became clear. Woodward and Bernstein, the journalists who broke the Watergate story, knew the facts. This man was the President and he had won his second term in a landslide, why would he need to engage in any criminal acts? Their gut instincts told them different. They felt something was wrong and in the end, their combined intuitive instincts led them to one of the greatest political discoveries of all time.

Now here are some big ideas to help you begin cultivating greater intuition:

Silencing the choir living in our heads

The choir living in our head is often a noisy and harsh inner critic that negatively judges us (and everyone else) nonstop. It has difficulty accepting that we are human and capable of talking ourselves into negative circumstances. Most of us experience this at some point. We criticize ourselves or worse, dismiss our perception of experiences in life as nonsense—not wanting to deal with the uncomfortable emotions that arise from events and situations and how they may impact us. It gets more hectic when we hold on to old, negative beliefs, bringing ourselves down with a tough, negative inner commentary. Let's be honest here: this won't go away just because we want it to. As the saying goes: old habits die hard, and this is one of the hardest to let go of. I like to say we are our own worst judge, jury, and executioner. So, what can we do when we recognize that we're our own harshest critic?

a. Create a list of the things you criticize yourself for. Are these honest criticisms? Do they have any basis in reality, or are they echoes of the negative voices you heard around you growing up? Then, ask yourself why are you constantly criticizing yourself? Where does this programming come from? Did someone teach you to disdain yourself? If so, what do you gain in life by holding onto this habit?
b. Take a one-day break! Even if it's only for a few minutes or few hours. Gift yourself an honest hiatus from your inner critic. Tell it to go on vacation. Write a small prescription for yourself that says: "inner critic is officially on vacation for . . ." Personally, it took me years of practice. And now I tell those negative inner voices to "shut up" and I do something more productive than listen to the monkey mind's song. (The other day a client referred to the endless drone of the inner critic as the 24/7 stream from K-FUK FM radio).

c. Practice reframing. This technique has been mentioned throughout this book and it's for a good reason. It works! When you hear that voice saying "nah, nah, nah, nah, nah!" Say STOP! You can say it a few times. STOP! Now, let's look at this issue differently. It takes practice but in time the technique works.

"Intuition is seeing with the soul."

~ Dean Koontz ~

Believe your experiences and question your thoughts

One of the ways we learn to respect our intuition and trust ourselves is by reflecting back on our experiences in a more honest, kind, and compassionate way. They're crucial to our health and wellness. But, how does one go about trusting their experiences? The key to trusting is to see them honestly and through eyes that are open and objective.

First, there's no way one can go about reviewing all of their experiences and reframing them all at once. Here are some ways to begin the process:

a. Make a list of 2 or 3 past experiences that still trouble you. Write them down. What happened? What was your role in the situation? Why do you think you criticize yourself for how this experience worked out? How can you look at the experience in a new way?

b. Meditate on the experiences. What might you do differently today? What has the experience taught you? Let the situation flow before your eyes with no judgments. Be an objective historian of your own experiences.
c. What were your physical reactions in these experiences? Did you have butterflies in your stomach? Did you have a gnawing at the back of your brain that told you "this is not right" before you entered into it? Very often our "physical self" will inform us in ways that our brains don't want to accept. For example, perhaps you're out on a first date. Things seem fine at first. Then, the other person says a few things that make you uncomfortable. You get a "sinking feeling" in your gut. Your body tells you something is wrong, but your brain doesn't want to listen. Those physical reactions are very important and part of our intuitive abilities.

After hours inner life

For centuries, philosophers, authors, academics, and scientists (and probably many others) have studied dreams, written about them, wondered why we have them. What do our dreams mean? There are many documented situations of people whose dreams accurately forecast events. How is that possible?

Dreams are a way that we can communicate and acquaint ourselves with the ideas and beliefs that exist in our unconscious minds. This makes a dream a tool that helps us to tap into our unconscious, revealing our true feelings about certain events, thoughts, or beliefs. When we pay attention to them, they can be

a guide to help our lives become more whole. And more often than not, our dreams will tell us what we're really feeling. They are quite connected with our gut instincts, something we may have severed ourselves from.

"It's hard to like someone you don't trust,
and it's hard to like yourself if
you don't trust yourself."

~ Leo Babauta ~

Life's Billboard Messages

Messages are found in the signs that come into our lives every day, dropping little hints about opportunities that may await us or things that we may be better off avoiding—not out of fear, but out of belief that it's not the right choice. Some call it the road signs of life.

One of the wonderful things about this exercise is how it allows you to make a thoughtful evaluation of things that have happened in the past. Can you recall an instance when you've said to yourself the signs were there all along guiding you on to the path or decision that you should have taken? Perhaps you didn't pay attention to them because it's not the truth you wished to see at the time or your focus was distracted elsewhere.

A personal favorite "Life's Billboard Message" occurred for me while standing at the airport baggage claim in New Delhi, India years ago during the fateful cycling trip that changed my life. The conveyer belt was going around and around and suddenly I saw some of my clothing strewn upon it. My suitcase came out after my clothing and upon retrieving the bag I discovered my favorite silk jersey cocktail dress had been taken. My mood was high as I was excited

to be in a new country embarking on the adventure of a lifetime but I was disappointed a favorite and expensive piece of clothing was stolen right then and there. In spite of my irritation I reframed the incident by telling myself that I hoped some lovely lady would be able to enjoy my dress and would deal with a claim to the airlines later. Then I chose to let it go because there was nothing else I could do about it at the time.

In hindsight, that incident was a message that I should have paid more attention to. Looking at the past through the rearview mirror I see the message that I needed to let go of my fancy life, my physical trappings and how I had defined happiness in the past in order to embrace the life journey that was ahead of me. It did not minimize my irritation but it does put the symbolism into perspective.

If only I had identified and embraced that message more clearly at the time I might have saved myself a lot of heartache in the years to come. I might have made choices earlier that would not have led to financial destruction and legal entanglements that we experienced.

We've all experienced those occasions when we've said to ourselves, *I knew that I shouldn't have done that. Oh well, too late now*. That thought cannot always be avoided, but it can be significantly reduced if we pay attention. For example, if you are disappointed that a friend cancelled dinner plans with you at the last minute and allow yourself to "mope" about it, you may not answer the call that unexpectedly comes from a long-lost friend out of nowhere that evening. Perhaps your friend's cancellation was nature's way of clearing your schedule to allow for an unexpected meaningful encounter? In other words, life is kinetic, constantly moving and shifting to accommodate both opportunities and challenges. I'm suggesting we pay closer attention to the signs not only for their meaning in the moment but for the context they provide that gives us a sense of the bigger picture of our lives.

It's time to consider what signs of guidance have been in your life and how you responded to them. These are examples of "Life's Billboard Messages." Learn to recognize future signs of guidance and omens by writing down past experiences—the ones you caught and the ones you wish you had noticed and heeded.

Have you ever had one of "Life's Billboard Message(s)" that upon reflection now appeared to be an electrified movie marquee? Think about the times that were filled with synchronicities, symbols, or metaphors that somehow offered some guidance about a situation but you were not open or available to use the information. Conversely, there may be times that ultimately didn't amount to a whole lot, even though you recognized them and thought for sure they would.

Name some of the important messages or themes that you have experienced over the course of your life.

____

____

____

____

____

Did you listen to all of these messages?

O Yes O No

If you listened to the message(s), how did heeding them improve the quality of your life, and hence, the quality of your happiness?

____

____

____

If you didn't listen to the message(s), how would have heeding them have changed your life for the better?

____

____

____

Would listening to the message have changed the course of your life?

O Yes O No

In what way?

____

____

____

"At times you have to leave the city of your comfort and go into the wilderness of your intuition. What you'll discover will be wonderful. What you'll discover is yourself."

~ *Alan Alda* ~

Trust Your Gut

"Your intuition knows what to do.
The trick is getting your head to
shut up so you can hear."

~ Louise Smith ~

Although it is often ignored, our intuition is something we should all be grateful for possessing—especially as we grow more accustomed to putting it to good use. It can guide us to good decisions and help us circumvent those moments in life that could negatively impact our well-being.

We learn a lot about ourselves through our intuition if we just take enough time to listen to it. Everyone has intuition, but some people are more in tune with it than others. Some people are oblivious to their intuition, but we *all* have an "inner-self" that is our intuition, or our inner guide. This is the part of you that knows the right thing to do in all situations.

When we choose to go against our intuition, we usually get into trouble. We all do it at times because we really want the treat that comes with taking the action, even though we know intuitively that the action is wrong. We all know when a person is lying to us or if they are a person we should not have in our lives. Yet we allow them into our lives because they are exciting or promise us something that we want. Of course, we always get hurt in the end because we didn't listen to our intuition. We knew better.

Rebecca's Story

As I sat down to write this chapter I recalled the story of one of the most resilient and intuitive women I have ever met in my life. Rebecca was in her early twenties and came from a "nice" family living in a coastal city along the northeastern seaboard. She shared this story in a group I facilitated shortly after checking into rehab. Her story will forever be emblazoned in the minds of the young men and women who witnessed her courageous recounting of what had happened to her and led her to that moment.

As a teenager, Rebecca became involved with drugs, prostitution, and notoriously bad gang members. Rebecca and her best friend were routinely physically, sexually, and emotionally abused by their pimp. One day the pimp aggressively beat up both young women and pulled them into the back yard of the house at which they were staying and proceeded to force them to dig two graves. The pimp shot and killed Rebecca's friend in front of her and forced her to bury the young woman. Before the pimp had the chance to kill Rebecca, she shared how she mustered the nerve and had a sixth sense that guided her to escape to safety.

A couple of years had passed since I had seen this woman but thoughts of her had been coming to mind recently because her strength of heart and character demonstrate how trusting our gut, sometimes without any good reason, can save our life or alter the course of it. Coincidently, the other day I had been thinking about her and walked into a local market and there she was. We hugged one another each with tears in our eyes. She had done it— she stayed clean, she saved herself, and was on the road to creating the life she desires.

"Intuition is always right in at least two important ways;
It is always in response to something.
It always has your best interest at heart."

~ *Gavin de Becker* ~

The questions that follow are meant to help you evaluate where you're at in the "trust your gut" department. Don't worry if you feel that you're not up to par, because you're on a journey and training toward greater happiness and joy.

Do you often have a sixth sense or intuition about someone or something?

O Yes O No

Is your intuition usually right or wrong?

O Right O Wrong

Have you ever not listened to your intuition and wished you had?

O Yes O No

Do you think that if you had listened to your intuition that things would have turned out better?

O Yes O No

Why?

____

____

____

____

____

____

____

____

What lessons have your past intuitions taught you?

____

____

____

____

____

____

____

____

How do you think you will be happier if you were to trust your intuition more in the future?

Key #4: We cannot control life, only ourselves

We don't have control over life's circumstances, only how we relate to them. When you focus on the big picture instead of a specific negative experience, you can stay dialed into the goodness that surrounds you, instead of temporary sadness, anger, or frustration. If you think big, you can move forward. You can persevere, instead of letting your dissatisfaction bog you down and make you stagnant.

“One can have no smaller or greater mastering than mastering of one self.”

~ Leonardo da Vinci ~

Happiness is a mysterious thing. We all want it, we all crave it, and still, we can't always have it no matter what we do. Although advertisements try to convince us that if we take the right pill we can be happy all the time, that's simply not true. Because life *isn't* always happy. This sounds harsh, but it's the truth. Happiness doesn't naturally spring up from beneath our feet each day. And that's because life isn't perfect. In fact, it can be downright cruel and unreasonable at times. And that's okay, because no matter what life throws at us, we have free will and we can use it all to our advantage.

Stuff happens. Every second many are born and many die. Life is filled with tension, disappointment, trauma, illness, and struggle as well as pleasure, excitement, satisfaction, beauty, and simplicity. Life is a “wiggly” experience. It moves this way and then it moves that way, often at the same time as happiness is regularly tinged by difficulty. Life is bittersweet.

How do you wiggle? How do you deal with the roller-coaster ride of life? How do you deal with hardships? Do you go with the flow or do you fight the tide?

When things go wrong, do you play the victim and engage in pity parties that don't serve you? I'm a big proponent of allowing myself the space and opportunity to acknowledge as well as feel what's happening, perhaps gripe about it a bit, comfort myself to the

best of my ability with healthy strategies then move on. Wallowing is nothing but a stew that gets thicker with time. Or do you realize that you have the power to control your expectations, your reactions, your choices, and yourself?

Simply, it comes down to practicing internal control instead of attempting external domination.

What does that mean? It means we can't control the people around us and we can't control events that happen around us. All we can control is ourselves. We can choose what we do, what we say, and most important, how we feel. When we exercise self-control, we realize that not only are we able to create a life of happiness, but a primary reason why we aren't happier more often . . . well, because we're not making that choice.

We don't want to hear that, do we? No one does. But stop and think about that for a minute. The thing that's holding us back from being truly happy is . . . ourselves. Chances are, you have probably begun realizing this by now.

You already know that looking outside of yourself for happiness hasn't helped. Many of us—including myself—can gain all the outer trappings of a "good life" but still not feel happy inside. You may have even tried scratching the surface of yourself to discover the cause of your unhappiness, but perhaps you stopped before digging too deeply.

And why? Because we don't really want to take full responsibility for our lives.

Let me clarify: Taking responsibility for our lives isn't about making ourselves feel bad and wrong about the choices we've made or criticizing ourselves as if we were terrible, weak, or a bad person.

We all have to stop that insanity right now. Think about this: when we realize that while we are not always responsible for the events that take place in life, *we* are responsible for our reaction/behavior and relationship to things not working out the way we would have liked. This is a very liberating concept because we then discover that *we* have the power to change things. Reminder and fact: by embracing this, we regain the personal power to change our perspective and transform our life course!

"Our deepest fear is not that we are inadequate. Our deepest fear is that we are powerful beyond measure. It is our light, not our darkness that most frightens us. We ask ourselves, 'Who am I to be brilliant, gorgeous, talented, fabulous?' Actually, who are you not to be? . . . Your playing small does not serve the world. There is nothing enlightened about shrinking so that other people won't feel insecure around you."

~ *Marianne Williamson* ~

Yes, you're the one who can turn things around.

And when you do, the only person you'll have to "blame" for your success is *you*. That does not mean we don't outsource the support we need from friends, family, mentors, and guides, but ultimately it is our actions that change our reactions to what has happened. I think of all the people who support me on my journey and have made it possible for me to be where I am now. And that's something to be proud of. You can stop getting in your own way by learning how to master the way you interact in the world.

The only control you truly have is over your own responses and reactions to the external world—in most cases, you can't actually control the issue you're forced to deal with. Do you think you can control the weather? Do you think you can control the government? Do you think you can control your partner's carnal desires? (Well, maybe a little of that last one.)

Even though you may possess the best parenting skills on the planet, do you think you can control your child's destiny? Do you think you have the power to singularly stop war, famine, political despotism, or economic disaster?

Many of us truly believe that we have the power to control everything in our lives. And we think that if we just work hard enough, we'll be able to change the world around us and bend it to our will. There's this thought in our minds that we are the only ones in the universe who matter. We're the *only* ones who can do anything about what's happening around us. And that's true and untrue at the same time. Can you change your world?

The answer is *no* and *yes*. You alone cannot cure the ills of the world. You cannot declare and enforce world peace, although that would certainly be nice. But you can change yourself, and the effect of even a simple personal change can have a tremendous impact on your personal happiness and even the world. But instead of focusing on mastering ourselves, we oftentimes try to control everything and everyone around us. We think that if we control others, we have power. And if we have power, we are happy. Right?

But total control over others is an illusion. Even if you can control what someone else does, like a parent controlling a child's schedule, you can't control how that person feels or thinks. In truth, no one can exert absolute control over anyone else—not even dictators. Nelson Mandela is a prime example of someone who lived in a prison for 27 years yet never surrendered himself to the degradation that was heaped upon him. Because he exercised mastery over his own reaction to his harsh circumstances, he forged a quality of character that helped bring an enormous shift to the country of South Africa. More important, no one likes to be controlled—not your spouse, kids, friends, or coworkers. Probably not even you.

But you do have a choice: you can take control over yourself and your own life.

In order to be the CEO of a company, one must be resilient enough to handle all the responsibilities, stresses, and day-to-day crises that arise. Otherwise, the entire company may fall apart because the CEO sets the tone. The CEO is the leader. Your mind is the CEO of your life. It's also where the choir of critics lives. And it's important to remind ourselves that we're not our thoughts and we're not our feelings. We are more than all of that. If you are unable to bounce back from a negative experience, your mind, body, and entire existence will suffer. This is an important distinction between who we are *and* the mind/body vehicle we embody into and need to learn to master. To live a happy life, your positive capacity to cope with everyday stresses and unexpected catastrophes is instrumental.

Managing the facts and emotions of a crisis is integral to surviving it. A crisis can stir many emotions including shock, fear, anger, misdirected action,

sadness, uncertainty, despair, and even paralysis. By developing good coping strategies, one develops resilience and the ability to gradually move forward in life to a new "normal." Coping doesn't mean ignoring your pain. It's okay to feel pain, shock, and fear. Just as a CEO will conduct a thorough assessment of his company after a negative financial quarter, you must assess your life to find the source of the negative emotions you are feeling. Find their root. Learn from them. And then let them go. I often ask clients, do you want to be right or do you want to be happy? Even the most cynical laugh and get the point. This too becomes a practice. Choose joy and contentment over sorrow and righteous indignation.

"If you don't like something, change it.
If you can't change it, change your attitude."

~ Maya Angelou ~

The world is not conspiring against you, no matter what it might feel like some days. On the days when you think everyone is trying to irritate you and make things more difficult, stop and take a deep breath. Stop personalizing the behavior of others.

We live in a time where victim consciousness is prevalent. We believe that we are suffering because someone else has caused it. Continuously, we look outside our minds and our hearts to find someone to blame so we don't have to take responsibility for anything. We're prone to see ourselves as victims, someone who others should pity and unquestionably support.

Most of the time, however, you aren't a victim of anyone else's wrongdoing. While there are certainly moments when you might suffer at the hands of someone else, in most cases, the only person who stands in the way of your personal happiness is . . . well . . . *you.*

When you continue to blame everyone else for your missteps, you create a situation in which there is always something or someone else that prevents you from being happy. You're having a bad day? Well, your partner wasn't nice to you when you got up, so that put you in a bad mood. And then the kids were screaming at each other, so they obviously hate you and want to make you suffer. And that brings up the belief that you're not a good parent, which in turn implicates your parents' perceived imperfect parenting of you.

Can you see how this creates a cycle of blame and a cycle of trouble in your life? There will always be someone in your life that isn't doing what you want him or her to do. No matter how great your life is going, there will *always* be someone you can try to blame for not being happy. But since you can't change the way other people behave, why not change the way that you react to their behavior? Can you look within and see if you did anything to provoke the situation? Can you do anything to fix things?

If you think about the way you normally respond to a difficult interaction with another person, you probably fall into a pattern of thinking:

- It's all their fault.
- It's definitely not my fault.
- Why do they always do this to me?

When you choose to be in one of these mind-sets, there is no room for you to take personal responsibil-

ity. Since you aren't the one to blame, you don't have to make any changes. But if you think this way, your personal happiness will always be contingent upon the actions of those around you. This irrational belief actually dilutes your power and gives it away. Pretty scary thought, right?

The truth is, you are in charge of how you respond to a situation. For example, if someone cuts you off in traffic, you can choose to become angry and to shout a few choice words out your window as your blood pressure surges up. *Or* you can choose to stay calm and wish the best for that person, for he certainly must be in a hurry for something. You have a choice. You are in control.

Here's something for serious consideration—not making a choice is actually a choice. It is willful inaction. Passivity is just as much of an action as taking a step.

Every moment of every day, you have a chance to ask yourself what you want to think and how you want to feel. Do you want to be right or do you want to be happy? Once you understand that you actually always have a choice, albeit active or passive, you will begin to better see how much power you really possess. If you find yourself obsessing you have been taken out of conscious awareness and could consider an opposing action to regain your power and control. What I mean by this is engaging in an activity that distracts your attention from your own busy brain (focused on a past event or one that has not happened yet) and ground the awareness in your body (think exercise, dancing, meditation, martial arts, etc.) which is present, always with you, and absolutely the only place that can offer you peace when your mind is behaving like a runaway train. Another option is to focus your attention and effort somewhere else where you and your rumination are not the star attractions (think community service and helping others). When we are behaving like master ruminators we must practice a different routine to achieve a different result. What I'm suggesting is that our conscious awareness becomes increased and our choice muscles strengthened. Once you're no longer at the mercy of those around you, you can begin to make decisions that are in *your* best interest. When you make your own choices, when you take control over your own life, that's when happiness starts to blossom.

This doesn't mean it's always easy or that you'll always make the right choice in a given moment or that you'll always feel good. What this does mean, however, is that you become responsible for your own life and that sense of self-control and emotional maturity is a really good feeling even when we're feeling down. Don't give others the power of determining whether or not you will be happy; it's not their job.

Your happiness is your job. And it's time to start taking it seriously.

You can take responsibility for your happiness by taking control of your actions and your reactions. And once you do, the world around you will begin to shift. The opportunities for happiness will become tangible because by taking control, you've empowered yourself to take advantage of them.

Make the choice today. Your happiness is waiting.

"Freedom is what you do with what's been done to you."

~ *Jean-Paul Sartre* ~

How Resilient Are You?

"Life doesn't get easier or more forgiving,
we get stronger and more resilient."

~ *Steve Maraboli* ~

Distress tolerance, our ability to handle discomfort and difficult situations, is intricately linked to how we deal with life's more challenging moments. We will have them, but it's how we manage them that really makes the difference. It takes work. As we strive to become more emotionally fit in order to increase our *H-Factor* we will need to become more resilient. One of the hallmarks of happy people is that they have the ability to bounce back after bad things happen. As I mentioned earlier, happy people do not have less misfortune in their lives than unhappy people. They just have a hardier character than their less happy counterparts.

Most of us have some level of resiliency hardwired into us, and at the same time we also have the power to strengthen our hardiness through training.

How do you handle life's rollercoaster?

Researchers share that, in general, resilient people accept the fact that life comes with disappointment and pain. In general, most people are stronger, gutsier, hardier, grittier, more adaptive and resilient than we initially believe ourselves to be. When it gets right down to it we rise to the occasion in order to handle crises, misfortunes, hardships, and tragedies.

And when trauma happens or the unthinkable occurs our sense of safety, stability, and foundational grounding are shaken to the core. Examples such as the premature death of a child, the suicide of a best friend, divorce, the fire that destroyed the family home, the spouse who received the terminal diagnosis, or the uncovering of marital fidelity all undermine our well-being and challenge our happiness often to the breaking point. We don't think we'll ever bounce back or that we will ever know happiness again. Most of us find a new level of normal after trauma but some of us become stuck, paralyzed and mired in the events that become our identifiable story (like a badge or medal). We can feel that recovery and healing are impossible and therefore, just not in our cards. This is tragic and it does not have to be this way. In fact, our ability to find more compassion, peace, and grace are virtuous qualities often born during the storms of life.

One of the powerful tools I use in working with clients' trauma is to ask them to make an honest assessment of what happened rather than denying or rationalizing the situation. I gently guide them to understand how wallowing in self-pity or a prolonged sense of victimization can be reframed into something much more helpful and constructive. This does not

mean we deny what happened, by-pass our emotions, and minimize the impact of the trauma upon our lives. Part of the healing demands that we begin to see the adversity as an opportunity for growth, transformation, and transcendence.

From time to time I reflect upon the personal and collective traumatic adversities our world has faced and will continue to face. I don't live in that realm on a daily basis but I do think about the men and women with whom I sit, witness, and listen to while holding space with unconditional positive regard and utmost respect for their journeys as well as the dignity of the process of their healing.

Over the last decade, we have all been affected in some way or another by the economic and natural disasters shared throughout the globe. Terrorist attacks, war, catastrophic earthquakes, domestic tornados, floods, and economic turmoil have caused many families to lose their homes, jobs, and even loved ones. Some of us have been lucky enough to be observers on the sidelines of these situations, praying for the speedy recovery of those less fortunate.

Although we never wish for traumatic experiences like these, I am always amazed to see the resilience of the human spirit in the people who undergo such tremendous circumstances. After suffering through extreme grief, anxiety, and anger, it may seem easy to just give up. But, these brutally honest introspective moments allow us opportunities to re-evaluate our lives, deepen our personal relationships, more fully appreciate life, and discover new talents within us previously unexplored.

If you have experienced the loss of a loved one, the financial burden of unemployment, or the loss of your home, you know that the grief can be unbearable. But, it is in the moments of our greatest sadness that our hearts are broken wide open. We let our walls down and become vulnerable. It is that same vulnerability that allows our hearts to soften, turning our thoughts to one another, and strengthening personal relationships if we allow ourselves to do so.

We are not meant to endure our pain alone because humans are a tribal species by nature. We are hard-wired to rely upon one another for support and to be connected to each other. It's in our DNA.

With these difficult changes, our priorities and philosophies often shift, and if we are humble in our reactions and mindful in purpose, our eyes begin to see hidden capabilities within us that can lead to a new path of joy. If we as individuals and members of society, apply our newfound strengths to productive pathways, we not only survive our difficult moments, but we do so with more grace and enthusiasm to overcome our past circumstances, help others do the same, and pursue options never considered before for personal development in a post-traumatic world.

We are survivors. It is within each of us to persevere and in the process discover we are so much stronger than we ever realized. With perspective, compassion, and love, painful experiences can lead to personal growth, greater empathy, transformation, and ultimately, renewed happiness. Post-Traumatic Growth is the potential silver lining of our worst nightmares if we can allow the process to unfold in truth, authenticity, and with support of one another. It's how we mend our hearts, minds, and souls into a more beautiful and whole person than we were before.

Remember the concept *kinsukuroi*? Our lives are like the Japanese ceramic process to "repair with gold." When a ceramic article breaks, the pieces are not discarded. An artist puts the broken parts back together with precious materials such as gold or silver dust mixed with the lacquer. Not only does it fix the object, it repairs it with greater strength and beauty than it had prior. The flaws and cracks are not hidden. They are exposed and embraced with the added texture that creates a richer history. Humans possess the same capacity, to become more beautiful, hopeful, and strong because of having been broken and then healed.

The blowback of war and trauma

Although the "D" would have you believe otherwise, Post-Traumatic Stress Disorder is not a one-size-fits-all medical condition. A Veteran who develops PTSD because of war trauma has a fundamentally different —though equally serious—experience of PTSD than someone who suffers PTSD after a car accident or violent attack. It only follows logically, then, that a Veteran would receive different treatment. Right? If only.

As more Veterans develop PTSD, we must resist the urge to treat this disorder with a cookie cutter solution. Through mission-driven coaching, we can augment and support treatment that is tailored to a Veteran's unique war-related trauma and can help our Warriors thrive with their minds, emotions, hearts, and souls more fully engaged.

The "D" in what is known today as Post-Traumatic Stress Disorder came about in 1980, when the American Psychiatric Association first classified PTSD as an anxiety disorder. This designation is undoubtedly a good thing: it's paved the way for funding and treatment options for the millions of Veterans and civilians living with these invisible wounds. It also has legitimized the significant struggles of people with PTSD and reaffirmed to the world that this disorder is not merely a case of someone having a rough time coping.

Understanding the medical seriousness of PTSD is crucial to knowing how to react to and treat this condition. However, let's not forget that there's another important element to the PTSD equation: the human one. PTSD has numerous physical and biological manifestations, but it also affects the heart and soul. Our treatment should embrace all of these aspects of the person who is suffering, not shun them.

To treat Veterans' PTSD, the Department of Veterans Affairs (VA) often administers several types of traditional psychotherapy including medication and Prolonged Exposure Therapy. Considered the traditional PTSD therapy, PET consists of 10 to 12 sessions in which a Veteran recounts the traumatic incident over and over until he or she can report it back step-by-step in great detail. The goal here is to have the Veteran be able to deliver the story much like a journalist would —unbiased, sharing only facts, and completely devoid of emotion.

For some Veterans, this process really can help them remove the trauma from the troublesome war event they've experienced. For others, though, reliving the event merely retraumatizes them. This process is hit or miss. And then there's the vulnerability aspect that comes when Veterans realize this information is now part of a permanent record that could keep them from getting a job or VA benefits down the road. The VA is in a tough bind, dealing simultaneously with a

lack of resources and a spike in PTSD diagnoses that run the gamut from minor to severe. The VA's efforts to establish a PTSD treatment program for our Vets are a step in the right direction. However, I'd like to propose a more holistic PTSD treatment model.

As more Veterans come to me seeking help for their PTSD, they often describe how the PET treatment brings feelings of stigmatization, fear, and desensitization. After this experience, they are unsure whether any treatment will truly help them overcome their invisible wounds of war and allow them to still feel human. That's where coaching-based support comes in.

A coaching-based PTSD recovery support program is based on solutions. Unlike PET, it's not training with one concrete mental goal in mind. It doesn't ask our Veterans to banish their feelings. Instead, coaching takes into account all aspects of our Warriors—mind, body, soul, and emotions—to help them engage in creative problem solving that will enable them to map out a route to achieving their goals. There's no stigma, no "who, what, where, when, and why," and no exercises designed to purge all emotion from our Veterans. The goal here is to empower through emotional growth, not cause the emotions to disappear.

Coaching is mission-driven, making it a lot like military training. This aspect of coaching focuses on training for the goal of optimal functioning making it particularly compatible with the mission-driven spirit of military service personnel. Being a coach is not being a shrink. It's helping our Veterans take back control of their lives—a process that helps reengage all the virtues and character traits that allow our

Warriors to deal with war situations. By treating the whole person and providing a unique mission-driven team approach, coaching promotes wellness after war that truly has our Veterans in mind—physically, mentally, and emotionally. When incorporated into a multidisciplinary treatment plan including meditation, psychotherapy, yoga, canine companions, anger management, addiction rehabilitation, equine therapy, and in some cases, medication, coaching offers our Vets the best chance to turn their trauma into growth.

Another perk of the person-centric coaching model is that it can be provided virtually or in person. To assist Veterans in underserved areas where there might not be easy access to PTSD counselors, Harvesting Happiness for Heroes has developed the R.E.B.O.O.T. program. Through these online community coaching sessions, we provide Veterans with stigma-free, integrated combat trauma recovery programming that allows them to embrace their emotions in a new, positive way rather than shrink from them.

I have the great honor of working with some of our valiant Military service men and women. Our Military is comprised of very smart and well-trained men and women. They naturally use humor to cope with the possibility of pending disaster. That is very much the Warrior's spirit.

My strategy when working with Veterans or anyone else who has suffered extreme trauma (think of a mother who has raped both of her sons and a father who beat them) is to validate and normalize their experience by pointing out that PTS is a normal reaction to exposure to abnormal stress. In my view, it is essential to remove the "D" from "PTSD" because the symbol of the "D" and diagnostic code of a disease or

disorder stigmatizes, pigeonholes, and limits opportunity to move beyond its name. It is also essential to explain the physiological responses to trauma including fight or flight impulses, adrenaline and cortisol (stress hormones) dumping, roles the amygdala (reptilian/primitive brain), pre-frontal cortex, mid-brain, hippocampus, etc. all play in PTS (and addiction) triggers and management. Once people begin to understand how their body is responding to triggers they can begin to learn ways to gain control back. PTS is longer the runaway train wreck but a set of conditions that can be harnessed, managed, and redirected. Hence, once the experience of trauma is honored and the mechanics of it understood, the stigma is lessened and the work required to heal can begin.

Another important component is the built-in mindfulness skill of a soldier. They are trained to be extremely mindful. They learn how to be fully rooted in the present moment on the battlefield because their lives depend upon it. The lives of their brothers and sisters in arms (inter-connected) depends upon it. Once that is illuminated for the Vet, they get it and usually can begin to learn how to translate that skill back into civilian life.

"Be kind. Everyone you meet is fighting a great battle."

~ *Philo of Alexandria* ~

Stress Tolerance and Happiness

"The greatest weapon against stress is our ability to choose one thought over another."

~ *William James* ~

Thoughtful evaluation of how you handle the stress in your life is a necessary part of increasing your level of happiness. We cannot always manage what happens to us; however, we can manage how we respond to it. Some situations are ones we've gotten ourselves into, while others just come our way. Our responsibility lies in our relationship to our decisions and actions moving forward. The questions to ask are: "What are we going to do about it?" And "how are we going to show up for life?"

Take a few minutes to think about how you view the following stressful situations. There is no need to write anything down. Simply become more aware, as that is the first step to mastering your response to the "unwelcomed" and and allowing your conscious awareness to help guide you through. Our ability to cope

with life's ups and downs can be influenced by several factors including our self-care. Are we eating, exercising, sleeping, and resting well? If we are not caring for and keeping ourselves well then we will be even less equipped to deal with unexpected stressful events.

- **Serious Problems**
  - Money problems
  - Family problems
  - Health problems
  - Children problems
  - Spouse problems
  - Job problems
  - World problems
- **General Life Frustrations**
  - Automated telephone recordings
  - Offshore telephone banks
  - Not getting to talk to a human
  - Understanding that human's accent
  - Getting disconnected after 2 hours of trying to get to the right person
  - Traffic
  - Missing a plane connection
  - Standing in a security line at the airport
  - Losing your luggage
  - Ordering take-out food and then discovering the order is wrong when you get home

Our First World problems seem challenging to us a lot of the time. If we're fortunate, we can take a moment to pause and maybe even laugh at ourselves. Is that extra minute that we wait in line really that significant? Or that light that we don't make it through before it turns red—will it really impact our lives negatively? Of course not! But consider this, if you're on a deadline it might. The tardiness could also save us from an accident. Being aware of how we respond to these small, unavoidable things can save us a great deal of unnecessary aggravation.

Of course, we'll have times when we are stressed by our situations. This is when it's important to see how to use that stress as a positive catalyst, not something debilitating. Maybe to avoid it you become more organized so you aren't running late to begin with. That's right. It's not other people's fault that you are running late for work and didn't make that light. Our degree of reactivity is significant in our lives because this type of low tolerance can be the onset for more significant problems with our health, possible addictions (coping), trauma, and our overall mental health.

It takes just a few select times of exercising control over our emotions to become more empowered by them. That does not mean we ignore what we are feeling. It means we acknowledge what is happening and then move forward seeing that our entire day doesn't have to be ruined by getting cranky at that person who is going five miles under the speed limit, instead of your standard five miles over it.

In order to raise our distress tolerance, we must become better adjusted to dealing with our own discomfort, displeasure, and disappointment. We do this by keeping realistic perspectives on the issues, managing expectations, taking responsibility for changing what we can, and surrendering the need to control what we cannot. In dealing with our suffering, the same methodology would apply. We acknowledge the issue, evaluate our role in it (past or present), and then make choices that allow us to live more comfortably and realistically with what is happening right here, right now.

How High Is Your Self-Esteem?

"You have been criticizing yourself for years,
and it hasn't worked.
Try approving of yourself and see what happens."

~ *Louise L. Hay* ~

Our stress tolerance impacts how we feel about ourselves as well as the situations and environment we find ourselves in. That means that it is also linked to our happiness with our relationships. Good relationships and life perspectives stem from healthy self-esteem.

Self-esteem dictates most of our responses to every situation, including the stressful. This means that it is directly tied to our level of happiness. Learning to love and accept ourselves for who we are, flaws and all, is *essential* to our everyday happiness, plus our mental and physical health. It's all a part of this one word we all want to feel: satisfaction (with a genuine smile and a happy heart).

Where does self-esteem start? Much of it comes from our childhoods, specifically from our parents and primary caregivers.

How our parents, caregivers, family members, and important authority figures treated us is directly linked to the self-esteem we carry into adulthood. Fortunately, if our self-esteem is suffering, it does not have to be a permanent condition.

Ask yourself the following questions:

- Do you ever feel depressed?
- Do you ever feel anxious?
- Do you ever feel stressed?
- Do you suffer from stress-related illnesses like headaches, stomachaches, insomnia, or fatigue?
- Do you ever feel angry or hostile to others for no particular reason?
- Are you distrustful of others?
- Are you competitive even when you aren't in a contest?
- Are you ever abusive to your spouse, parents, or child?
- Are you experiencing abuse from some other person?
- Do you have addictions to alcohol or drugs?
- Do you have an eating disorder?
- Do you feel shy and nonassertive?
- Do you feel aggressive?
- Do you always feel defensive?
- Are you overly critical of yourself? Others?
- Are you ever sarcastic?
- Are you promiscuous?
- Are you overly dependent on another person?
- Are you codependent with another person?

Codependent relationships are a type of dysfunctional helping dynamic where one person supports another person's addiction, poor mental health, immaturity, irresponsibility or under-achievement.

> "Codependency is a psychological condition that is manifested in relationships. Codependents give a great deal more love, care and respect (LRC) from others than they expect, request and ultimately receive. Even though codependents are resentful and angry about the LRC inequality, they do not terminate the relationship. In the event that they or their partner do end the relationship, codependents perpetually find themselves on the giving end of a new relationship."
>
> *~ Ross Rosenberg ~*

- Are you overly sensitive to criticism?
- Do you ever try to put on a false front to impress other people?
- Do you feel like an outsider looking in, in social settings?
- Do you ever feel lonely?
- Do you feel as if you are an underachiever?
- Are you always obsessed with your problems?
- Do you feel you have a lower social status than others?
- Do you feel that you are a worthwhile person?
- Do you feel that you are a failure?
- Would you rather be you than someone else?
- Are you fair with yourself by acknowledging both your strengths and weaknesses as part of a balanced whole?
- Are you happy with your physical appearance even on a "bad hair day?"
- Do you know your flaws and accept them? Or do you exaggerate them in your estimation and condemn yourself for them?

Increasing your self-esteem through positive self-care

Once we are aware of what our obstacles are in regards to self-esteem, it is time to work on increasing it. There are mentally and physically healthy ways to increase our self-esteem levels making every day an opportunity for greater well-being. A baby step a day becomes significant over time and will build a greater level of emotional comfort in your life.

The four pillars of good self-care are strong mind, body, spirit, and emotions. Below are some great ideas to get you started. Some will be listed several times, as they are wonderful for more than one of the four components. The important thing is to commit to taking the first baby step and then another and another. Practice makes permanent! You will notice overlap in some areas because many of these simple interventions work on multiple levels to help boost self-esteem.

Mind

- Meditation—starting with 5 minutes a day and building up from there try focusing on your breath, a word, a phrase, the sounds of nature, or the stillness
- Deep breathing, you already know how to do this but in this case allow yourself to be still and attentive to your breath
- At least eight hours of sleep per night, more if possible
- Being mindful of making better decisions for yourself
- Increasing your resilience by become more willing to extend the length of time of your focus

or tolerance of minor discomfort in small doses trusting that it will pass and you can endure. Simple examples would be meditation or exercise, both of which may be distasteful or uncomfortable at first but neither will kill you and both will get easier, perhaps even pleasant with time
- Trust, test, verify, and repeat

Body

- Aerobic exercise: at least 30 minutes a day
- Weight training
- Yoga or Pilates
- Stretching
- Healthy eating habits: nourish yourself with high-quality foods that fuel health and healing
- Weight management
- At least eight hours of restorative sleep per night
- Trust, test, verify, and repeat

Spirit

- Operate from a place of gratitude
- Meditation, prayer, or contemplation
- Being of service to others
- Embrace a sense of spirituality that works for you
- Write or find and prominently display uplifting statements, poetry, prayers, or mantras
- Trust, test, verify, and repeat

Emotions

- Building self-esteem by acknowledging how your actions positively matter

- Address your feelings instead of burying them
- Increase distress tolerance to build emotional muscle-tone
- Read uplifting passages from poetry, prayers, or inspirational texts
- Trust, test, verify, and repeat

As you to treat yourself with love, respect, honor, and decency by practicing positive self-care you will slowly notice a shift in how you feel, think, act, and look. Take note of the changes. They are the proof of trusting the process, testing the interventions, validating that shift is happening and repeating the cycle over and over again to make transformation a habit. One of the many gifts that come from being able to authentically soothe and support ourselves is that it becomes easier to extend this loving action to others.

"It's surprising how many persons
go through life without ever recognizing
that their feelings toward other people are
largely determined by their feelings toward
themselves, and if you're not comfortable within
yourself, you can't be comfortable with others."

~ *Sidney J. Harris* ~

Key #5:
Our happiness is our personal responsibility

Guess what? It's your own responsibility to be happy. There's that word again: responsibility. When you think about happiness, the last thing you might think of is the idea of being responsible for it.

“People who learn to control inner experience will be able to determine the quality of their lives, which is as close as any of us can come to being happy.”

~ Mihaly Csikszentmihalyi ~

“Okay,” you say. *“Lisa, I’ve read this far in the book and I’m thinking about what you’ve written. I am beginning to see that what you are telling me about creating happiness in my own life makes sense. I guess I will muster a little faith in myself and attempt to put these tools to work.”* First of all, thank you. Faith is a big deal, and it’s something that doesn’t come easily for many people, especially when they don’t personally know the person they are putting their faith in.

Faith is important. Faith is the condition in which you allow a belief to guide you, even when you have no proof that your thoughts will make any difference in your life. You just have the faith in your heart, and you move in the direction it leads you. It’s scary . . . but, it’s necessary.

But what does faith have to do with happiness? More than you might realize.

As poet Kahlil Gibran once explained, *“Faith is a knowledge within the heart, beyond the reach of proof.”* Faith is the fuel that powers the engine of hope. It is your deep, unwavering belief that your hope is connected to the universe and is actually capable of making things happen. If you don’t have faith to support your hope, all you are doing is crossing your fingers and wishing for the best. And since our greatest hope

in life is for happiness, faith is one of the greatest tools we have to achieve it ever more often.

That doesn't mean that having faith will eliminate all fear, nor would we want it to. Fear can be a tremendous motivator and can be used to promote transformation. The problem with fear comes when it paralyzes us, causing us to do nothing with our life.

All of us have doubts and fears, but we don't have to let them stop us from living the life we want to live, from doing the things we want to do, or from having the happiness we know we deserve. You deserve to be happy, no matter who you are and no matter what has happened in the past.

Sustainable, authentic happiness is unconditional and ongoing in your life. It is like a seed that is planted, cultivated, and slowly grown over time. You water it, you nurture it, and then you see the plant emerge from the soil. You continue to care for the seed, making sure it has enough sun, enough water, and enough nutrition. And even though that plant might die someday, you know how to grow another.

Unlike happiness, which takes time to cultivate, joy is a far simpler state of being. You don't have to do anything or become anything to experience it. It comes from accepting and embracing what actually exists in this very moment, for this moment is all that we know for certain.

Look around you. Think about your life in this very second. This is what you can count on. Everything can change in an instant; you cannot count on what will happen an hour from now, let alone a day, month, or year. Only now matters. If you find your mind anywhere but here simply stop and take inventory of your senses in the present moment. What does your body feel like now? Are your feet grounded? Is your breath relaxed and steady? Can you feel your clothes kissing your body? When we take the time to slow down, we reduce the speed of everything racing in our heads and redirect our bodies to presence. Presence is a free gift absent of judgment and pregnant with limitless possibilities. When we are present we are agreeing to show up for life fully and wholeheartedly to experience a state of being rather than our typical thinking and doing.

And when we fully occupy our lives here and now, there is no space to ruminate about the past or worry about the future. The present becomes the most hospitable place to reside for our well-being.

Faith and spiritual practice are measures of belief. While you don't have to believe in a certain deity or religious practice in order to have belief, believing in something is important, even if that means you just believe in yourself. In fact, that is the most important belief. Belief is repetitive thought and if we have the ability to harness and manage thought then we have the skill required to believe. Science, however, backs the notion that those having a strong spiritual practice live happier and more fulfilling lives. Connecting to something greater than ourselves invites us to be a part of the universe and not focused myopically on being the center of it. Spiritual practice can take on many forms beyond religion.

Why is it so important to have faith in yourself? Because when you have faith in yourself you can trust in the moment you are in—even if it appears to be a disaster. In fact, there is nothing you need to fear. Faith is actually the *acceptance* of fear and agreeing to act in spite of it. This means we have courage to be

in the moment and accept the present, come what may. This does not mean we have to like it. It means we agree to be with what is present and respond to it consciously. When you have faith, you can focus on what is before you, and you can respond to what you need to respond to with relative equanimity rather than frightened reactivity.

As you read this, where are you now?

Are you are here in the moment, focused? Or are you distracted by the things that surround you? If you are distracted right now, you're not the only one. We live in a society that offers distractions each moment of the day.

What could be distracting you from being happy here and now? Texting, e-mails, online shopping, social networking—all of these things are just fillers wasting your time while distracting you from attaining your true happiness.

Turn everything off. Disconnect. Focus on the right here and now and think about what you are feeling. Sometimes, this can feel a little too much, which might be why you turn to technology to distract you in the first place. When you're distracted, you don't have to think about how and what you feel in the moment because your energy is focused elsewhere. The devices can become a barrier to connection with what's really going on inside. You can skip right ahead to the future or hop back in time to the past. That's called digital distraction and it's one of the most easy and accepted ways we numb our emotions.

Ruminating about history with regret or projecting fear about the future are happiness killers. These actions take you out of the experience you could be having *right now*. The moments we all casually pass up will never happen again. Never. No moment will ever be exactly like this one.

Stop, breathe, and slow down your mind. Remember *where* you are. Remember *who* you are. Think about what you want. Today, you can be happy because you make a choice to be happy. Believe that you are worth the time, the energy, and the effort. Because you are. Because we all are.

"To be is to do."

~ Socrates ~

Isn't happiness something that just occurs?

Not quite.

Even the people in your life who seem to be 100% happy are working hard every day to ensure they continue to be that way. True, they might make it look easy, but that is because their choice to be happy is ingrained.

And yours can become that way too.

Let's talk about happiness right now. It may be hard to acknowledge this, but *only you* are responsible for making yourself happy.

Your partner isn't responsible for making you happy. Your friends aren't responsible for making you happy. It's all up to you. And this makes sense, since you're the only one who knows what you need to feel happy. That is, if you've taken the time to discover your happiness.

Figuring out what makes you happy isn't a simple task, especially if up until now you've relied on others

or superficial things to make you fleetingly happy. You might have to try out a few different things before you find the recipe for your own personal happiness and contentment.

Allow yourself pleasure. This can be a challenge especially if we don't think we deserve it. However, doing small things that bring us pleasure validates our worthiness and boosts positive emotion. Begin each day by simply asking yourself what you can do to support your own happiness?

Ideas might include engaging in simple pleasures, things like making yourself a flavored coffee. Or something more extensive like:

- Fitting in a time for meditation
- Going out to exercise
- Making time for a favorite hobby, like playing the piano or taking photographs
- Taking a class such as cooking or sailing
- Considering an alternative career path

In time, you'll begin to see that there are plenty of ways to support your happiness with simple actions that have a very positive effect on you and your life.

But your happiness isn't always going to make everyone happy. At least not at first. We know that change is hard to embrace for ourselves and when others perceive shifts in us it can challenge or destabilize their sense of familiarity and upset the status quo.

When you begin to take control of your own happiness, you'll notice that your loved ones or colleagues might be confused by the changes in your behavior. You're changing the way things have always been, and you might not be meeting the expectations of those around you. By putting yourself and your happiness first, you might have less time to invest in other people's needs and happiness. And you know what? That's okay.

While in the past, you might have focused on trying to make everyone else around you happy, the new you is taking a different approach. And that's a good thing. Because the happier you are, the more you will have to give to others.

What you're doing right now is akin to putting on your own oxygen mask while on an airplane in distress before helping anyone else around you. You can't help others if you don't take care of yourself first.

Of course, it might take time for the people in your life to adjust. Your partner, your friends, and your family might call you "selfish" for taking time for yourself to do things that make you happy. And that's okay. Being selfish is actually okay. Because you're not hurting anyone with the things you're doing. In fact, the better you take care of yourself and your happiness, the better partner, friend, family member, and professional you will be.

If you notice that people around you are having trouble adjusting to your new way of life, it's a good idea to talk to them about why you're doing what you're doing. Most of the time, they'll start to understand once they hear that you're choosing to be happier.

Because who's going to tell you to stop being happy? No one. Happiness, and the quest for sustainable well-being, are contagious. And that, my friend, is why seeking your personal happiness is in the best interest of your family, community, and the world.

When we make changes in our lives by investing in our happiness, the people around us will start to

wonder what they can do to become happier, too. And when this happens, when everyone starts taking responsibility for his or her happiness, the joy in the world will grow exponentially because happiness is an unlimited resource: as long as we seek to cultivate it in a socially responsible way (without infringing on the happiness of others), there is no limit to what can happen as a result.

"The universe is change; our life is
what our thoughts make it."

~ Marcus Aurelius ~

The Willingness to Feel

"Knowing yourself is the beginning of all wisdom."

~ Aristotle ~

Part of happiness is intricately linked to how we allow ourselves to feel in any situation. It can be easy for anyone to wallow in negative thoughts and feelings—even more so than to savor the positive ones that come our way. In fact, negative thinking was essential for our ancestors' survival. This is called "negativity bias" and our brains are built to be more sensitive to bad news or potential threats in order to help us avoid danger.

There are also those who are unable to identify and put emotions into words. This is an actual disorder called "alexithymia" and 10% of the population suffers from it. When this unfamiliar but common disorder is acknowledged, therapies can be recommended to enhance:

- Emotional awareness
- Social attachment
- Interpersonal relationships

In order to be emotionally fit we must be willing to participate in the feelings that we do have and not avoid them. And all of us are challenged to create happiness and positive outcomes from even the most difficult experiences. In fact, we can use life's challenges to grow stronger, more resilient, and happier. It comes down to giving ourselves permission to feel whatever is going on for us at any given moment.

The notion of the "willingness to feel" might sound a bit like an oxymoron. After all, don't we all feel something all the time? The answer is: unfortunately not. Many of us engage in numbing behaviors (as mentioned earlier) and many of us find other ways to feel as little as possible. We rely on our intellect such that the decision-making process becomes something purely objective with as little "gut instinct" involved as possible. We might ask ourselves "why would we pursue a life devoid of feelings, or feel only the surface of our experiences?" The answer is in the experiences themselves. Many of us have been scarred by abuse, trauma, dysfunctional families, or horrifying relationships that seem to suck the soul out of our lives and rob us of happiness. The willingness to feel is ultimately about opening ourselves up to the possibilities that surround us—the emotional possibilities of life. As Walter Last writes:

"Feelings are the builder of the body, the glue that holds body and soul together. Tender feelings make us open and vulnerable. In order not to get hurt, we prefer to close up and not to feel. This has the added advantage of making us stronger in our career, because we do not need to take our feelings or the feelings of others into consideration.

Each time we suppress a feeling or do not express it in a suitable way, the generated energy solidifies into muscle tensions. Eventually, this leads to widespread muscle armoring, a permanent state of muscle contractions. This closes off the circulation of blood, lymph, bio-energy and, equally important, the flow of feeling energies."[1]

Oftentimes it's more difficult to feel the truth of a situation. For example, when someone we love dies it's agonizing when we actually feel the loss of this person. Still, if we try to run away from our feelings they will only catch up with us one day. Then, it will be even harder to deal with because we've denied our feelings for so long.

Many of life's experiences can and will challenge us emotionally—such as:

- Being laid off from your job
- Having a child leave or return home
- Dealing with the death of a loved one
- Getting divorced or married
- Suffering an illness or an injury
- Getting a job promotion
- Experiencing money problems
- Moving to a new home
- Having a baby

Suppression of our emotions is not like they glorify it on Star Trek where Mr. Spock is an enlightened individual who knows how to control his emotions and live guided by his logic alone. It can lead to a wide range of physical problems such as:

- Back and/or neck pain
- General aches and pain
- Headaches
- Sweating

- Weight gain or loss
- Sexual dysfunction
- Shortness of breath
- Dry mouth
- Anxiety or panic attacks
- Insomnia
- Upset stomach
- A compromised immune system

When we are in touch with our feelings, we can feel the internal changes that help us to become a better person, parent, and partner. Our emotions in any given moment are genuine and if we do not deny them, we allow ourselves to process them. In turn, we don't set up as many obstacles in our path to happiness and our lives become better because we are fully embracing what comes with "living." It takes trust and courage to access feelings and this is something that we all have the ability to nurture. As we learn to self-soothe and self-regulate our emotions we take another step toward self-mastery and happiness.

"You must learn one thing:
the world was made to be free in.
Give up all the other worlds
except the one to which you belong.
Sometimes it takes darkness and the sweet
confinement of your aloneness
to learn
anything or anyone
that does not bring you alive
is too small for you."

~ *David Whyte* ~

Tears and Fears

"Nothing in life is to be feared, it is only to be understood.
Now is the time to understand more
so that we may fear less."

~ *Marie Curie* ~

Fear is one of the most powerful persuaders that our minds have. It can dictate so much, including often being the source of what we choose to ignore about our given feelings. We've learned great insight into why we need to address our feelings and the value of doing so. Now it's time to get to the source of much of the chaos—fear. When we manage fear, we manage to free ourselves from an emotion that can become crippling to us in many ways. Fear impacts our choices, our lives, our freedom, and our ability to try new things.

Former U.S. President Franklin D. Roosevelt said it best, "The only thing we have to fear is fear itself."

A rapidly changing society also brings about a sense of fear in many of us. Think about it . . . In the

uber-fast world we live in, a cell isn't just something in our body; it's also a type of phone. A tweet isn't just the music of a songbird; it's an integral aspect of social media. Everything is transforming around us so quickly we rarely have time to adapt to one new innovation when the next one is already "the new thing." Remember when 3D movies were changing the modern cinema? Now we have 3D television, but that's already a few years old. Whether we like it or not, uncertainty is the new normal. Everything around us is in constant flux. It's understandable that some people (perhaps many) would fear these constant changes. Fear is in fact a natural part of our lives. We're taught to fear some things (and for good reason), but oftentimes our fears begin to take over.

What if there was a way to turn the fear, anxiety (and self-doubt that rides along with it) into positive action in the face of uncertainty; the head-to-toe butterflies into fuel for brilliance? You can. We all can. We're all trainable. Everyone has the ability to learn new ways of doing things. We can either accept our fears, or we can work to transform them into something new and positive. When we activate our creativity, allow ourselves to be innovative, and engage in practical problem solving, we begin to transform fears into fuel for change.

In a famous series of novels, anthropologist and author Carlos Castaneda wrote that the Nagual (Sorcerer) was chiding him for always writing down such meticulous notes. During one conversation, the wind came and blew all of Carlos' notes away. The Nagual laughed and said, "You can either allow the wind to blow you any way it wants, or you can ride the wind to where you wish to go." In that part of the story, the Nagual imparted great wisdom to his student. We have the power of our choices. We can choose to be fearful, or we can choose to transform our fears into something more useful and more positive.

Here are some BIG ideas to help catalyze fear into positive change:

Reframe and rewrite your story

One way we unknowingly instill fear in ourselves is through the inner dialog that constantly runs through our minds. "I'm too fat," "I'm not smart enough," etc. The storylines we create around a particular feeling or experience are more determinative of success than the actual circumstance itself. They affect our willingness (and therefore ability) to act and the quality of any ideas or creativity of potential solutions we could manifest. Many of us are raised on negativity. It's all around us. That is an unfortunate reality. But, the good news is we can revise and update our mental script. We can rewrite our stories to be more meaningful and more positive. It is our thinking that paralyzes us with fear and not always the situation itself.

Reframing is an excellent and empowering process. It asks us to suspend those negative stories inside ourselves and explore the story from another perspective. This gives us a chance to reconstruct or reframe a new storyline; one that empowers us to experience an uncertainty not as a time for failure or inaction but for meaning, opportunity, and transformation.

A very popular and constant fear among so many is the question, "What if I fail?" Yes, we sometimes will. That doesn't mean we don't get right back up. Instead of creating a doomsday scenario, create a successful one. Change the question to: "How can I

recover?" or "How can I learn from this experience?" Then, we have a chance to build new stories. Failure can become a gateway for creativity if we change our relationship with it.

Practicing presence

A basic mindfulness practice couldn't be more simple: take a comfortable seat, pay attention to your breath, and when your attention wanders, return. If greater well-being isn't enough of an incentive, scientists have discovered the benefits of mindfulness techniques can help improve our physical health in a number of ways. Mindfulness can help:

- Relieve stress and anxiety
- Treat heart disease
- Lower blood pressure
- Reduce chronic pain
- Improve sleep
- Alleviate gastrointestinal difficulties
- Enhance focus
- Better manage emotions
- Bolster creativity

Some experts believe that mindfulness works in part, by helping people accept their experiences—including painful emotions—rather than react to them with aversion and avoidance. It's become increasingly common for mindfulness meditation to be combined with psychotherapy especially cognitive behavioral therapy. This development makes good sense since both meditation and cognitive behavioral therapy share the common goal of helping people gain perspective on irrational, maladaptive, and self-defeating thoughts and behaviors.

Mental fitness

We've all seen the research on exercise and health, weight loss, and disease prevention. But, did you know that certain approaches to exercise also have a profound effect on your brain? Daily cardiovascular exercise, for example, especially with high-intensity bursts mixed in can improve mood, executive function, decision-making, and creativity while decreasing anxiety and fear. The latest research even reveals the possibility that exercise can grow new brain cells, something that until only a few years ago was thought to be impossible. It's also strongly correlated with decreases in anxiety and elevation of mood, which are directly connected to improved creativity and problem-solving.

Embrace uni-tasking

Multi-tasking is out. Research suggests that our brains don't multi-task, they just rapidly switch or toggle between tasks, sometimes fast enough for us to believe we're doing many things at once. The problem is, every time we switch, there is a "ramping cost" in your brain, it takes anywhere from a few seconds to 15 minutes for your brain to fully re-engage. This makes you feel insanely busy, but simultaneously compromises productivity and creativity while increasing feelings of anxiety and stress.

Multi-tasking also requires you to hold a lot of information in your working memory, which is controlled by a part of the brain known as the prefrontal cortex (PFC). But the PFC is also responsible for willpower, and keeping fear and anxiety in check. Multi-tasking increases the "cognitive load" on the PFC, overwhelming it and effectively killing its abili-

ty to keep fear, and anxiety at bay. Simple solution—just say "no". Do one thing at a time in intense, short bursts.

Emotional Intelligence—developing smarter feelings

Emotional Intelligence (EI) refers to the ability to perceive, control, and evaluate emotions. Some researchers suggest that emotional intelligence can be learned and strengthened, while others claim it is an inborn characteristic. The notion of EI generally refers to possessing three integral skills:

- Emotional awareness, including the ability to identify your own emotions and those of others.
- The ability to identify, track, understand and harness emotions can greatly enhance how we think and problem-solve. Cognitive consciousness allows us to be more effective in creating solutions and resolving conflict.
- The ability to manage emotions, including the ability to regulate your own emotions, and the ability to cheer up or calm down yourself or another person.

A heightened degree of emotional intelligence has personal benefits. For example, increased self-awareness helps you respond better to day-to-day situations. Similarly, a heightened level of empathy can lead to a healthier response in one's interactions with others.

Start chasing zombies—turn the spotlight on your myths

We all carry certain myths about ourselves and others. These myths help to frame our sense of self, and importantly, our self-esteem. If we buy into these myths about ourselves and our life, then we are likely to allow ourselves to be bound by them. This will, in turn, lead us to limit the opportunities we try to open up for ourselves in life. We will have already accepted a pre-conceived notion of who we are and therefore decided well beforehand whether or not we will be successful in an endeavor.

The first step is to ask yourself what myths you have decided to accept about yourself? Some very common ones are: I can't do that, I'm not smart enough, or I'll never meet anyone; there's no reason to try because it won't work out anyway. Millions of people carry these myths inside themselves. The key to letting go of these is to break them down into small pieces of facts and reality. These myths can be transformed into these more positive statements:

- I can do anything I put my mind to.
- I am willing to try new things.
- I deserve and can enjoy a loving relationship.

Then, one has to back these up with actions. One of the ways myths take hold of us is they paralyze us from taking action. Once you write these down and keep saying them, follow up with the practical action steps you can take to make these happen. Our thoughts and attitudes can either be self-limiting or limitless and correlate directly with our ability to govern our lives.

Stop running, take one step at a time

Just like multi-tasking, some people fear change because they see that so many things in their lives need to change. There is no way anyone can change everything in his or her life at once. It's impossible. But, what *is* possible is to lay out steps for change by creating a calendar of action steps for moving forward. Practical thinking is one of the ways that we can dilute our fears and transform ourselves into agents of change. Here's how to do it: Write down the things you want to change and why. Create a priority list. What's most important? Why do you need or want to change this now? What feels like your most pressing need? What are you willing to do about it? How will you do it? When will you begin?

When we make a vow to engage in positive change, there is often that rush of emotion that excites us. We are no longer feeling helpless and frustrated. Yet, this can quickly change if we try to move too fast, or accomplish too many goals at once. Our fears have often been with us for many years and we can't simply erase them because we want to. It takes a concerted, committed effort of positive self-empowerment. There are several forms of psychotherapy that can be particularly helpful in this regard; one of them is Cognitive Behavioral Therapy (CBT). CBT focuses on the skills and strategies we can use for positive change in our lives. The emphasis is on working with the therapist, and then practicing the strategies at home between sessions. It can be extremely effective over time.

Embrace a path of change

As stated above, change is about commitment. It means that we must become passionate about transforming our lives. One cannot expect that transformation to come about quickly or easily. To embrace a path of change means to become dedicated to the importance and process of change in one's life. Here are six steps to aid in the transformation process by embracing change:

- Recognize that life itself is impermanent
- Reduce expectations
- Acknowledge change
- Accept change
- Learn from experience
- Be aware of your changes

When you set reasonable goals and don't expect or demand a particular outcome, you're better able to manage any changes that do come your way. Be aware that shift is constantly occurring. In fact, it's a guarantee. This means understanding that things can—and will—be different from how they are now. Acknowledging change is allowing it to happen when it unfolds instead of approaching change from a place of denial and resistance. Instead of resisting, allow change to flow and become deeply aware of what's transforming and why. Change is our greatest teacher, but only if we give ourselves permission to learn from it. Keep track of your changes in a journal, a log or on a calendar. Accept that change takes time. Embrace small steps that lead to bigger advances in your growth.

Take charge of your personal empowerment

Empowerment is one of those words that people like to say, and love to write about. But, what does it actually mean? The essence of self-empowerment is personal responsibility—taking full, complete control and accountability for your own life and circumstances. Here are the primary characteristics of self-empowerment:

- Having decision-making power of your own
- Having access to information and resources to make informed choices
- Having a range of options that you have determined for yourself
- Being able to exercise assertiveness in collective decision-making
- Having the belief in oneself to the extent that you feel you can make positive change, or have the ability to make change for yourself
- Pursuing personal growth that is constant and self-initiated

A person aiming for empowerment is able to take control of their life by making positive choices and setting goals. Developing self-awareness, an understanding of our strengths and weaknesses as well as exploring our perceived limitations is key to personal empowerment. It's also important to reiterate that many of our seemingly self-limited beliefs are based in myth and not reality. Sometimes we think we cannot do something, therefore we don't even try. And at other times we expend a tremendous amount of effort and still don't succeed. It's our most noble and best effort in pursuit of change that becomes the ultimate prize. Our best and most joyful lives can then be found in the journey, not the destination.

Amanda's Story

Amanda was a U.S. Military service member who was a truck driver in Iran. She was not directly on the battlefield but was most definitely on the frontlines as she was responsible for moving supplies about the country in the midst of war and chaos. Needless to say, she returned home after multiple tours of duty traumatized, exhausted, suicidal, depressed, and very poorly emotionally dis-regulated. Makes perfect sense after all that she had been through right?

The curious thing about her is that she missed the adrenaline rush of driving her big truck at high speeds while dodging enemy bullets and bombs. She had become an adrenaline junkie, which is very typical behavior of soldiers and first responders used to living life on the edge of death. Amanda craved the high octane charged emotional peaks that she felt as stress hormones such as adrenaline and cortisol flooded her body. She experienced a heightened awakened state of being alive while temporarily managing the fear of her risky actions in order to stay alert and safe.

As she transitioned back to post-deployment civilian life she would seek her adrenaline fix by driving the freeways in her hometown at dangerously high speeds at night to simulate her evening routine while deployed. Her high-speed adventures were haunted by Post-Traumatic Stress flashbacks especially while passing under bridges and overhead passes triggering the rush she got from defensive driving at high-velocity while in the war zone. She was completely alert and engaged but not present in the moment or her body. Her reptilian brain was telling her

she needed to escape a past danger not remotely existing in the present moment. She was good at it. However, the problem was her speed far exceeded safety limits and she would sometimes do it with her kids in the car.

Her challenge became recognizing safety, fully grounding herself in the present moment, and separating past experiences from present reality. Her terrified children became her reality checkers and reminded her to slow down. She had to radically change her behavior in order to avoid potential disaster, legal repercussions as well as potentially traumatizing her children. Unfortunately, second-hand trauma is often the unintended legacy we gift those we love.

I'm happy to share that Amanda possessed the courage to change the behaviors and heal the emotions that trumped her past fears. After intensive psychotherapy combined with medication she regained control of her life. She returned to school and became a licensed therapist in order to serve other Veterans challenged by PTS. Amanda was transformed by her war experience and transcended her challenges by making meaning out of them. Fear is not the enemy. Lack of courage to do something with fear is the Grim Reaper.

Each person's path to change is unique and an individual's pathway to transformation doesn't necessarily align with how another person approaches change. Everyone has their own fears and challenges. The time, commitment, and passion one brings to the transformation process will largely dictate how the process unfolds. The fears we hold, how long those fears have been in place, the ways in which the fears affect our lives, and the reasons why we hold onto them will certainly impact the process of letting them go.

The rhythm of change is something each person can feel taking place in their lives. As these fears dissipate, they are replaced with more positive thinking. The more one works on positive strategies, the less likely the fears will return. Change is a rhythm that has its own feel inside everyone. Some days will feel better than others, and some fears will be easier to let go of than others. But, it's the commitment that makes the difference.

By challenging and releasing our fears, we grant ourselves the insight and emotional freedom to do great things. We have free will and self-determination to change our perceptions and inner conditions, but doing nothing is also a choice we can make.

Inaction is also a choice. Choosing to do nothing and choosing not to change something that does not positively serve us is a sad misuse of our personal power. If you find yourself caught in a daunting loop of suffering and inaction ponder these questions: what benefit or secondary gain are you receiving from these conditions? Does your misery and discontent help you perpetuate a story or label that justifies your past or supports your present unhappiness? Would you be willing to contemplate that the story you are telling may be irrelevant to your present and future well-being?

"Courage is not the absence of fear, but
rather the judgment that something
else is more important than fear."

~ *Ambrose Redmoon* ~

Transforming Fears into Fuel for Change

"We generate fears while we sit. We overcome them by action. Fear is nature's way of warning us to get busy."

~ Dr. Henry Link ~

Name at least 3 fears you feel you're holding on to and why you do so:

1. ____

   ____

2. ____

   ____

3. ____

   ____

   ____

   ____

   ____

How can you begin to rewrite your own story in more positive words?

____

____

____

____

____

How can you begin to practice the art of mindfulness in your own life? Name 3 ways:

1. ____

____

2. ____

____

3. ____

____

How do you understand the notion of "embracing a path of change?" How can you do this in your life?

____

____

____

____

____

What myths are you holding on to that are potentially holding you back in life?

____

____

____

____

Name 3 ways you can begin a path of self-empowerment:

1. ____

____

2. ____

____

3. ____

____

Give 3 reasons why you want to embark on a path of change and letting go of your fears:

1. ____

____

2. ____

____

3. ____

____

"When people are ready to, they change.
They never do it before then, and sometimes they die before
they get around to it.
You can't make them change if they don't want to,
just like when they do want to, you can't stop them."

~ Andy Warhol ~

The Art of the Fine Whine

"Complaining does not work as a strategy. We all have finite time and energy. Any time we spend whining is unlikely to help us achieve our goals. And it won't make us happier."

~ *Randy Pausch* ~

Our emotions are not separate from the rest of us—they are an important part of how we perceive, experience, and interpret the world around us. In an article on the processing of our feelings, Dr. Barton Goldsmith suggests that sometimes we can't say everything we feel because of the nature of a situation. Other times, however, we need to express our joy, sadness, pain, or whatever we're feeling in order to cope with life at that moment. In this same article, Dr. Goldsmith offers this advice: "Being true to your emotions can't help but make you feel better about yourself, for you're able to be authentic." [2]

Whining is definitely part of complaining but it's more emotional and often involves a rather annoying tone that people define as whining. Sometimes we need to complain. We got laid off our job, or a client didn't pay, or our neighbor insists on holding late night jam sessions five nights a week. Modern life can weigh us down, but as the Chinese philosopher Confucius pointed out, it's often a matter of perspective. And perspective leads to action. The question here is; what can we do when we see ourselves becoming, or we have already become, a chronic complainer?

"Kvetch" is the Yiddish word for complaining. But, there's a nuance in the word that doesn't quite fit into a standard translation. It's more like someone who truly gets on your nerves. When we complain all the time, we risk becoming the kvetch; the person who gets on everyone's nerves. So, how do we detox ourselves from the dysfunctional pattern of complaining? How do we let go of the habit? Let's face it—sometimes a good complaining or whining session makes us feel good. Once it's over though, do we want to go on complaining, or do we want to do something about the situation?

Recently, a bright star in the world passed away—Dr. Oliver Sacks, a British neurologist and author. He received the news of his terminal cancer about six months before he died. He had time to complain and whine if he wanted to. Sacks wrote how he would love more time on earth. Instead, he focused on what he could still achieve in the time he had left:

"It is up to me now to choose how to live out the months that remain to me. I have to live in the richest, deepest, most productive way I can. In this I am encouraged by the words of one of my favorite philosophers, David Hume, who, upon learning that he was mortally ill at age 65, wrote a short autobiography in a single day in April of 1776. He titled it 'My Own Life.'"[3]

It has often been said that it's not what happens to us in life so much as how we deal with it. This is not to suggest we're not allowed to complain. Of course we are. There are medical benefits to speaking our mind in a healthy, blunt way, and we can create medical problems when we bottle everything up inside. The key is to find balance, a way to communicate in a healthy, self-honoring, and respectful manner as much as possible while still maintaining the possibility (and permission) that every now and then we need to have a good "rant." In fact, a timely "rant" can also be a healthy way to communicate or gas off and can be especially useful in the presence of a valued empathic, neutral listener. This allows us to feel seen, heard, and understood as we "let off steam." Another author and radio show host I know published a wonderful rant about second-hand smoke. She hates it, as do I. But, there's no point in trying to lecture every person you come across who smokes. You can, however, have a good kvetch about it and then move on.

Psychologist Dr. Guy Winch suggests that people often become chronic complainers because although they're aware that they complain a great deal, they feel their lot in life more than justifies their constant whining.[4] Even though people around them complain about the complaining, they might continue to persist because of their strongly held beliefs about their life's situation.

To help those of you who feel you may have fallen into the constant complaining mode of life, it's helpful to know just how beneficial life would be without this habit.

Here are some direct benefits of complaining less, complimenting more, and practicing consistently generous gratitude:

- A less negative attitude in life
- Happier and healthier relationships
- More energy
- More optimism
- Increased productivity
- Improved sleep
- Better overall life management

Here are some fantastic ideas to help you detox from engaging in a pattern of chronic whining, complaining or kvetching.

Chart or journal your pattern

One of the healthiest and most practical ways of letting go of any negative or dysfunctional pattern is to begin keeping a journal. Here are some tips for how to use the journal effectively.

1. **Keep an honest written list about whom you are complaining.**
   Are these colleagues? Are they family? Friends? Keep an honest log about whom you're complaining. How are these particular people triggering you? Are their behavior and your reactivity long-established patterns that no longer have any positive place in your life? For example, sometimes we hold on to friendships with people even though we no longer see them (except perhaps on Facebook) or even communicate with them that well. But, they've been in our life for a long time. Then, we fall into a pattern of complaining about them; about why we don't see them, about why we never hear from them, etc. Some people are in our lives for the long haul, and others for shorter periods of time. But, when we lose that connection,

it's tempting to fall into a pattern of complaining about it rather than taking action. Are certain situations troubling to you and all you do is complain about them? Again, chart the patterns. Find out which situations seem to trigger you more than others.

2. **Write down the kinds of complaining you tend to do.**
   Do some complaints become more emotional than others? Do some complaints tend to stay with you and keep bothering you over and over? Do you find you're saying the same thing repeatedly? When you see the way you complain, the words you use, sometimes you become aware that those words no longer have any meaning for you and you can stop the negative loop.
3. **Transform reactive into proactive.**
   At the end of each week take the complaints you've written down in your journal and see if you can transform your reactions into proactive ideas. Instead of complaining about that neighbor you don't seem to get along with, how about inviting them over for coffee and cake and talking about a positive solution? Change the dialogue. Rather than complain about the situation, focus on what you can do about the situation—how you can be neighbors together, how you can work together. Find your commonalities rather than what divides you. Journals have wonderful transformative abilities. Here are some direct benefits of journaling:

   - Helps to clarify your thoughts
   - Helps to empower you
   - Helps to strengthen you as a person
   - Helps to make you more self-aware

- Helps you speak your mind (contains your complaints and whines in a safe place)

Once you get into the habit of journaling, you may find it offers a wonderful contribution to your life. Some people journal their entire lives.

Reveal the pattern

Just as people can become addicted to harmful substances, abusive relationships, gambling, and other negative/dysfunctional patterns, we can become addicted to complaining. For some people it's about attention, for others it's a way of being heard in a world/life where they feel invisible and unheard. There are many reasons why people become chronic whiners and complainers. Edie Weinstein, M.S.W., L.C.S.W. writes about chronic complaining as another addiction:

"Complaints can also bond people . . . Complaining allows us to vent frustration and anger in safe, socially acceptable ways. It's good to unload rather than lug these feelings around. But complaining can become habitual or even addictive."[5]

When whining becomes a habit then it's time to understand the pattern and the reasons why. Complaining can be difficult to let go of when you don't understand what's underneath the pattern. Take an honest inventory of your life using the following questions: (think of this as a chronic complainer's survey form):

1. How often do I complain?
2. What do I tend to complain about?
3. Do my complaints have any basis in fact or reality, or are they emotional outbursts?

4. Do I tend to do anything about my complaints or do I just keep complaining about the same things repeatedly?
5. When do I do most of my complaining?
6. What are my biggest triggers? (people, situations, etc.)
7. Have I ever honestly tried to change the negative situation into a positive?
8. Am I willing to try and shift my thought patterns? If not, why?
9. Do the people around me complain a lot as well? (Do you associate with other chronic complainers?)
10. Have the people in my life talked to me about this and asked me to change? If so, how have I responded?

Once you've answered these questions, use these answers as a means to understanding your own thought patterns. Understanding ourselves is the first step towards change.

Take a vacation from whining and complaining

The path to healing involves being in touch with your decision-making process. Our choices are the greatest power we have in life. When we take charge of our choices rather than allowing events to randomly unfold, we proactively participate in our own lives. We begin to direct our life rather than being a passive observer. Once again, Dr. Guy Winch offers us some helpful advice about our tendencies to whine and complain:

"The problem is that today we associate the act of complaining with venting far more than we do with problem solving. As a result, we complain simply to get things off our chest, not to resolve problems or to create change, rendering the vast majority of our complaints completely ineffective."[6]

How about if you actually made a choice to stop complaining for a certain period of time? One can begin with a small period of time, for example, 2-3 days. Then you can build from there and go for longer periods of time. The primary problem with being a chronic complainer is that it sends us into victim consciousness. We become someone who feels powerless over our own lives. When we actively take a break from this behavior, we begin to release ourselves from the belief of being a helpless victim and start being fully accountable and responsible for our actions.

Here are specific steps you can take to begin the detox process of letting go of chronic complaining:

- Schedule a timed whining session. Give yourself permission to dump and then stop when the buzzer goes off.
- Approach your complaining for what it is; a state of mind.
- Realize you are using chronic complaining as a negative way of life and replicating old, dysfunctional dramas.
- Examine how your complaining can be confusing and hurting to people in your life.
- Learn to identify the triggers that provoke your complaints.
- Declare certain time periods to be "complaint-free zones."
- Forgive yourself, don't be hard on yourself, and recognize it's a difficult habit to break.

Effective fine whining in action

There are reasons to complain. Sometimes we're in a situation where we should complain. However, there are effective and ineffective ways of complaining, and it's important to know the difference. When we complain effectively we can actually have a boost in our mood and our self-esteem. Just as chronic complaining can damage our mood and self-esteem, the opposite is true. So, how does one learn to complain effectively?

- The next time you find yourself wanting to complain, ask yourself if this is something you want to change. If so, what do you want to do about it? Write down 2-3 possible solutions. Consider that if you skip the whining and complaining and go right to the solution you will have greatly empowered yourself. The next time will be easier and so forth.
- Complain at the right time. All too often we let something fester inside of ourselves. Then, days, weeks, or even months later, we explode. This is the opposite of effective complaining. Take the time to speak up. The longer you wait, the more likely it is that people will have completely forgotten the incident and have trouble understanding what you're talking about.
- Take ownership of your complaints. Rather than accusing someone else, use yourself as the foundation for the grievance. Rather than accusing someone, use yourself as the foundation for the complaint. This involves saying things like: "I feel," or "I experienced." This lets the person know that this is about your feelings and your

experiences rather than an outright accusation or personal attack.

- Do this in private. Take the person aside and have this as a private discussion. It's completely inappropriate to humiliate someone in front of other people. That will only create anger and resentment.
- Say what you need to and stop. It's not effective to lecture someone. It's not even appropriate. Keep your comments brief and to the point.
- Complain about the right thing. Don't use the time to bring up a string of complaints. Stay focused and clear.
- Always look for a positive solution—a way to end on a high note. Use the conversation to move forward rather than wading in a stagnant drama. Remember, the point of the constructive complaint is to find a positive solution.

"See if you can catch yourself complaining, in either speech or thought, about a situation you find yourself in, what other people do or say, your surroundings, your life situation, even the weather.
To complain is always nonacceptance of what is. It invariably carries an unconscious negative charge. When you complain, you make yourself into a victim. When you speak out, you are in your power.
So change the situation by taking action or by speaking out if necessary or possible; leave the situation or accept it. All else is madness."

~ Eckhart Tolle ~

Design a "letting go" ritual

Very often rituals enable and empower us to let go of things we have been hanging on to for no good reason. Sometimes we just can't seem to let go of that bad relationship, or that lost job opportunity, or that disagreement with a friend. We want to but can't seem to find a way to make it happen. So, instead of letting go, we whine and complain about it. *Why did that happen? Why couldn't that break-up have been nicer? Why does that friend continue to ignore me?* . . . Perhaps it's time to design a complaint ritual.

Here's one that may work:

- Write down all of your long-standing complaints. Make sure you're thorough in your descriptions.
- Read these complaints aloud.
- Take this piece of paper to a large body of water. You can say words like: "I now give myself permission to fully release these complaints from my life. They no longer have any purpose or meaning for me, and I let them go for my greater good." Slip the piece of paper into the water and watch it float away. As you do, allow yourself to fully feel that you are actually letting go of these complaints once and for all.

No victims only volunteers

As stated earlier in this chapter, when we allow ourselves to enter into a state of chronic complaining, we absolve ourselves of the responsibility to make our own lives something more positive. We let go of that responsibility and throw everything to the wind. This is surrendering to defeat by admitting we are powerless, helpless, and a victim of poor circumstances.

Complaining is a denial of responsibility. It's also a way of blaming others—like our boss, our family, our partners, our society for our personal situation. We blame them rather than saying, "I'm in charge. I'm the one who can make things happen for the better."

The question is; how do we turn this around when we've been in the blaming habit for so long?

- When you're in the beginning or even the midst of a complaint, STOP. Ask yourself: "Do I really want to be doing this?"
- Turn the situation around. Reverse the pattern. Say things like: "This is in my power to change. I take responsibility for this situation and what I wish to do about it."
- Allow yourself time to focus. Sit down. Take 6-10 deep breaths. Have a cup of tea and think. This is a good opportunity to give yourself a "time out" and simply breathe. Give yourself several minutes and allow your mind to clear. A solution will present itself. If you're at work, then sit at your desk quietly (or perhaps there's a quiet room?). Close your eyes and breathe deeply.
- Ask yourself: "What do I need right now?" Let the answer come into your awareness and guide you.

Exit the pity party

Let's face it, pity parties can be fun. We're all sitting around feeling sorry for ourselves. *I can't meet anyone. I'm never going to be happy. My life sucks. The world is a horrible place. And so on, and so on . . .* We should be honest here. Sometimes life does suck. Right? You've gotten bad news from the doctor. A relationship has broken up or you might have lost that great job oppor-

tunity you really wanted. It's all too easy to open the fridge, pull out that pint of chocolate chip ice cream and drown our sorrows in a feeling of self-pity and the sweet taste of comfort. Of course things will never get better. Here's the truth—they won't get better if you're absolutely convinced of this as your reality.

One of the people I admire is Dr. Bernie Siegel, the famous doctor who has worked with many folks coping with cancer. He famously told the story where he worked with a patient who told him the specialist declared he only had a few months to live. Dr. Siegel replied that the patient could live as long as he wanted and shouldn't pronounce a death sentence over himself. Ten years later the person was still alive and ran into the specialist. The specialist was shocked and told him he should have died a long time ago. A few days later, he did. Siegel strongly believes that our attitudes and our mind and our body are one.[7]

What does this have to do with chronic complaining? Everything! We can sit and cry over a cancer diagnosis, or react as Dr. Oliver Sacks did—be grateful for life and keep living. Pity parties are one of the unhealthiest events we can attend—even if we add decorations and great food, the outcome is the same. We sit around feeling sorry for ourselves. So, get off the sofa, and exit the party. Throw the ice cream away and find an empowerment opportunity where people get together and focus on the ways in which we can enrich our lives, not feel sorry for what we don't have.

Identify all the usual suspects

Okay, who are your major complaining partners? Who are the people you know who just love to complain?

Let's narrow this down: are there specific people you just love to whine and complain with? Evaluate these questions:

- What are you complaining about? Do you gather around the water cooler with your colleagues and complain about work? The boss? Your salary? Again, make a list of your general complaints. Then, begin to focus on solutions. Unhappy about your salary? Try negotiating with your boss. If that's not a possibility, consider a different job.
- Why are some people on the list and not others? Do you consciously avoid people who don't complain, or those who tell you they're tired of your constant complaining? If you're avoiding these people, it's time to learn why.
- Once you've made a thorough log of whom you complain with and matched them to the types of complaints you share, reflect on these questions: How did these complaining patterns set in? How long has this been going on? It may be time to change who you hang out with, or perhaps time to transform the nature of these relationships from negative to positive.

Feed your empathy gland with compassion

This is one of the most beautiful and positive strategies we can have in our personal toolbox.

First, ask yourself these questions:

- Am I complaining about people I actually care deeply about? If so, remind yourself that everyone goes through their own difficult times.

A friend of mine likes to say, "We all have our own bag of troubles." All too true. Remember, we don't always know what's going on in someone else's life. Our bosses also have their own problems, their own bag of troubles to handle. Perhaps their partner is ill, or they have a child who copes with autism, etc.

- Do I truly take the time to understand others? Often our complaints are based on an incomplete understanding of a situation. But, we keep on complaining and we don't stop to learn all the facts. Get the facts and focus on those rather than an emotional response to the situation.

Try to think of the other person in a situation. For example, in a car accident. Even if the other person is at fault, remember, it's likely they feel absolutely horrible about the situation. They might be dealing with fear, shame, guilt, and a whole host of feelings. Feeling empathy for them can be a hard leap sometimes, but one that's definitely worthwhile.

Practice the art of empathy. Express compassion and dispense love as it softens the blow of the ongoing challenges we are all facing.

Let go of the "I" focus; it's we, not me

All too often our lives are completely focused on ourselves. We live in a time of technological innovations that provide instant gratification. We can download movies instantly, watch concerts on the Internet, listen to music constantly on our iPods, and find whatever we want to buy online 24/7. But, what about the outside world? One of the most positive strategies for letting go of constant whining, complaining, and kvetching is to move away from the "I" focus.

Here are some tools to help:

- Get involved with your community: serve on a committee at school, or at your church, synagogue, mosque, etc. Show the community that you care about them and learn about the world of needs outside of yourself.
- Do volunteer work: There are hospitals, community centers, libraries, nursing homes, hospices, and so many other places that need you. Go online to your own city's volunteer board and you'll find a world of opportunities.
- Spend more time with family and friends: It's just possible that you've begun to isolate yourself and tend to live inside the world of all your complaints and concerns. Have you begun to distance yourself from others? Now's the time to reverse the pattern.
- Find an issue you care about deeply and get involved! Do you care about climate change? Women's health? Children's issues? Seniors? Then find a way to do something. Instead of complaining about climate change, volunteer with an organization devoted to positive change.

"Everybody in the world is seeking happiness—
and there is one sure way to find it. That is
by controlling your thoughts. Happiness
doesn't depend on outward conditions.
It depends on inner conditions."

~ Dale Carnegie ~

Emotional Vampires and Mental Bloodsuckers

We may encounter people who will either drain us emotionally or make us feel like we have no energy left to even focus on the positive aspects of our lives. I refer to these people as emotional vampires, or mental bloodsuckers. If they are a part of our daily life, we may brace ourselves before we know we will see them. They could be that boss that we always feel is out to "get us" or even a tumultuous relationship with someone we love, such as a spouse, parent, or child. All we know is that it seems unlikely that we will communicate well with them when we interact. In essence, we already "assume" that the interaction will be more negative than positive.

I have compiled a cute and curiously true survey to help you identify the toxic people that you may be allowing to sabotage your happiness. While it might not be possible to get every single one of these people out of your life—who would be left anyway?—it is possible to get the worst happiness-robbers out of your life or at least limit your time and exposure to them, *even* if they are in your family. Once you have discovered who these people are and how badly they are affecting your life and well-being, you'll want to explore some effective ways to extricate these people from your life in order to create more freedom, peace, and contentment.

Do you allow people into your life that make you feel bad about yourself?
- O Yes O No

Do you allow people into your life that complicate your life?
- O Yes O No

Do you allow people into your life that sap your energy?
- O Yes O No

On the left, write down the name of the toxic person in your life. To the right, next to each name, write down how you perceive they make you feel bad about yourself, how they sap your energy, and how they complicate your life.

__________ ______________________________

____

__________ ______________________________

____

__________ ______________________________

____

__________ ______________________________

____

__________ ______________________________

____

__________ ______________________________

____

Now write down how *you let* each Toxic Person affect your happiness.

Person: ______________________

____

____

____

____

Person: ______________________

____

____

____

____

Person: ______________________

____

____

____

____

Person: ______________________

____

____

____

____

Person: ____________________

____

____

____

____

Person: ____________________

____

____

____

____

Do you now take responsibility for allowing all the toxic people in your life or all the time you spend with them?
○ Yes ○ No ○ Uncertain

Now, write down what *you* can do to get *each* toxic person out of your life or to limit your exposure to that toxic person as much as possible.

Person: ____________________

____

____

____

____

Person: ______________________

____

____

____

Person: ______________________

____

____

____

Person: ______________________

____

____

____

Person: ______________________

____

____

____

Person: ______________________

____

____

____

Now that you have identified the toxic people in your life, do you plan to immediately get them out of your life?

O Yes O No O Unsure

If you can't get a toxic person or persons out of your life because they are family or you work with them and you can't quit, do you have a plan to limit your time with them?

O Yes O No O Maybe

How do you feel eliminating toxic people—or at least limiting your time with them—will now add to your well-being?

____

____

____

____

____

"If you have time to whine and complain about something, then you have the time to do something about it."

~ *Anthony J. D'Angelo* ~

Key #6: Choose activities and people that foster happiness

Do something everyday that makes you happy. Your life is filled with places into which you can expand your capacity for love and happiness. You don't need to hold it back. Happiness isn't something that needs to be limited to how you feel. Love and happiness can be a part of your life in all of the tasks you handle, mundane or challenging though some might seem.

"Let the beauty of what you love, be what you do."

~ Rumi ~

Perhaps happiness used to be something that was hard for you to define. But now; as you've begun to cultivate it, maybe you're feeling a little more hopeful and experiencing glimmers of greater optimism that ignite more love for yourself and life. Happiness, like love and laughter, is the best medicine.

Who do you love? What do you love? Your partner, your children, your family, your friends, your work, your hobbies, your body, your mind, your gifts as a human? How about yourself, just as you are, and life, just as it is?

Often, we spend a huge amount of time and effort loving other people or things, but we forget that true happiness actually starts with the self. It begins with loving who we are, loving life, and wanting to live life in full bloom, in full-spectrum color, and out loud, while everyone is watching (and even when they're not). And when you love yourself, you will be happier. And when you are happier, the people around you will be happier too.

This is because, as you now know, happiness creates more happiness. And this is not surprising. A law of physics states that an object in motion will stay in motion until an equal and opposite force acts upon it. This means your happiness will continue to expand as long as you don't stop it. Your love for life will continue to grow, as well—as long as you don't stop that either.

- Do you love nature? When are you going out for that hike, stroll, bike ride, fishing or beach trip?
- Do you love to cook? When are you going to plan that special menu, prepare your favorite dish, or create a celebratory environment in which to enjoy this meal?
- Do you love your work? When are you going to initiate that passion project you tucked away years ago?

When you begin to realize that happiness creates more happiness, you can see the value of creating happiness in everything that occurs in your life. When you have a happy work life, this will allow you to feel more creative and to be more successful, which encourages you to be happy at home and with your friends, which inspires you to try a new class or a new skill . . .

Are you starting to see the potential? The possibilities? They are endless.

Every day, do something to make yourself happy. Prioritize, organize, and execute it. Don't wait until you feel down or sad before you make happiness a priority again. Being happy requires intention, attention, and action on a daily basis.

Intention is the statement that you *intend* to be happy in your life. When you state this aloud, it becomes a promise you've made to yourself to make changes that will support your intention.

Attention is being aware of the ways that you support—and don't support—your intention. When you focus your attention on your progress, you can make adjustments to the way you live your life to accommodate your intentions.

If you want happiness, manifest it by planning for it. Bring this intention to your attention by taking action. Don't just sit and hope that happiness will show up at your door. Imagine if you wanted to find the love of your life but you closed yourself off from having a social life by staying home and even avoiding online social networks. That doesn't seem like a good plan, does it?

Intention + Attention + Action = Change

Do something each day to feed your senses. Read something uplifting. Cater to and delight your inner child by eating dessert first. Listen to beautiful music. Allow yourself to laugh and experience wonder. Nurture your body with healthy food and exercise. Meditate. Feed your mind, body, and spirit with healthy nutrients.

Sometimes, crystallizing your intention can be accomplished by engaging in a symbolic ritual or act.

For example, take a walk into your backyard and start weeding. As you pull away the pesky weeds and rooted vines that strangle the life out of the precious flowers in your garden, think about the weeds you can pull out of your life. Bad habits, unsupportive friends . . . weed them out. Get rid of the guilt, judgment, excuses, and feelings of unworthiness.

Get rid of the feelings that have held you back and that have stopped you from pursuing your true happiness. Get rid of the old stories you have told yourself. Choose to eliminate irrational beliefs and outmoded behaviors.

Each time you see something in your life's garden that doesn't belong, ask yourself what value it has for you. If it's not serving a positive purpose in your life, reframe this belief or remove the situation completely.

Choose to pull it out by the roots and throw it away. And if it returns, as weeds often do, then deprive it of the "water" of your attention by focusing on what it is you do want rather than putting energy in opposing what you don't want.

You're making space for the good things in your life again. Still, it's not enough to just remove the "weeds" that don't serve you. What new seeds can you plant to contribute to your future happiness?

Here's a simple happiness challenge: set aside one hour a day to do something that makes you happy. One hour may feel like a lot of time, but your well-being is well worth the investment. Sure, we might all say that we're too busy, but that's just an excuse. We must make time for ourselves because when we do, we invest in our well-being and that improves the quality of our lives.

Sow the seeds of joy, cultivate your crops,
and reap your harvest of happiness.

Now that you've been working on taking responsibility for your happiness, it's time to start bringing more happiness into your life. Right now. Not tomorrow, not on Monday. Now.

Right now, stop and think about how you're going to fill up that hour you are going to spend on yourself every day. Remember, you don't have to use it all up at once. (For example, it could be fifteen minutes, four times a day.)

Here are some ideas:

- Meditate
- Exercise
- Take a hot bath
- Cook your favorite dish

- Read a book
- Listen to music
- Learn something new
- Play
- Sing
- Color
- Garden
- Knit

You get the idea. Think of ways that you can support your happiness every day. Happiness shouldn't be something that you think about once in a while. You need to be more active in creating your happiness—and that means you need to include something that makes you smile every day. It's important to mention that authentic happiness is not a goal. It is the positive gift of your journey. Happiness is the by-product that happens naturally when you do more of what you love or do what you are already doing with more love.

Some days, it will be easy to find something to do. Other days, you might struggle because you're under a lot of stress, you're sick, or life does what it does best—creates the unexpected.

Even then, find ways to make yourself happy. Even if you worry that others may perceive that what you're doing is silly or strange, do it anyway. This isn't about them or their judgment. This is about you and your happiness. If you feel like wearing a cocktail dress or tuxedo to lunch because it makes you feel glamorous or suave, do it. If you want to take up line dancing or ballet at the age of forty-six, do it. If you want to write a screenplay (even though you have zero experience), do it. If it makes you smile, don't question it. *Do it.*

This isn't about asking others to define your happiness. This is about *you* and you alone. What can you do each day to make yourself as happy as possible even when life is not always happy?

Now do it. I know you want to.

"The present moment is filled with joy and happiness. If you are attentive, you will see it."

~ *Thich Nhat Hanh* ~

Emotional Housekeeping

"Emancipate yourselves from mental slavery,
none but ourselves can free our minds!"

~ *Bob Marley* ~

When we view our mind as a beautiful garden we understand that one of the things that is not welcome in that garden is a weed! They take over quickly, choke the healthy roots and become the negative focus, instead of what is good for us emotionally. That's when it's time to do some serious mental closet cleaning in order to make space for something better.

Cleaning out the cobwebs, dust-balls and poorly fitting beliefs is not always easy. It's a liberating process and the work of a lifetime. However, as we lighten our load, we feel enlivened and amazingly fresh and free, while wondering why we didn't do this a long time ago. Imagine this undertaking like spring-cleaning. To begin, you must first identify the emotional clutter that causes the unhappiness in order to "let go" of it. Explore the following exercise that will help identify and analyze who and what you are allowing to sabotage your life and what you can do to stop it.

Name three or four emotions, people and/or situations that you refuse to let go. This includes anger, hard feelings, judgments, disappointment, and negative attachments. Everything! Next to that write down how your life would be happier if you let this person/situation go. Then write down one thing you can do to let go of that feeling.

1.____________ ______________________________

____

____

____

2.____________ ______________________________

____

____

____

3.____________ ______________________________

____

____

____

4.____________ ______________________________

____

____

____

Let go of unrealistic goals and expectations by coming to terms with your own limitations. Create goals with identifiable steps that you are capable of achieving. Redefine your goals to make them more within your reach. Many people talk themselves out of doing things as if they were unrealistic given current circumstances. Yet that may just be a self-limiting belief. Question if the goal is realistically challenging or not possible at this time.

Write down three or four goals that you would like to achieve in your life. Next to each goal write down if they are realistic or unrealistic. Next to that write down how you can alter these goals to be more attainable and less frustrating. Managing expectations while making steady progress (not perfection) are hallmarks of successful and happy people.

1. ______________________________

____

____

2. ______________________________

____

____

3. ______________________________

____

____

4. ______________________________

____

____

Let go of negative behavior by acknowledging those unproductive actions and replacing them with positive behavioral changes.

Name three or four negative self-limiting behaviors that you know you have or that you have been told that you have. Next to each behavior write down what positive behavior you can substitute in its place.

1. ______________________________

____

____

____

2. ______________________________

____

____

____

3. ______________________________

____

____

____

4. ______________________________

____

____

____

Let go of old negative attitudes.

Write down three or four restrictive negative thoughts that keep you small, stuck, and constantly pop up in your mind. Take each negative thought and replace it with an opposing positive thought and action.

1. ______________________________

____

____

____

____

2. ______________________________

____

____

____

____

3. ______________________________

____

____

____

4. ______________________________

____

____

____

Let go of old hurt and pain by disowning and releasing old thoughts, ideas, and people that are no longer an asset to your life or your highest good. Replace bad memories with good ones. Review and reframe negative events from the past as positive catalysts that allowed you to achieve something desirable or served you well in some way.

Write down three or four bad memories that you hold on to. Next to each bad memory, replace it with a good memory or life lesson as a result of that person or situation. If there is no good memory or life lesson, replace it with a good thought or memory of something that you enjoyed about that time in your life.

1. ____

2. ____

3. ____

4. ____

Let go of preconceived ideas of how you think your life should be by finding joy in what your life is now. There are likely judgments you have held about yourself, those around you, and the world at large that have kept you separated from finding and creating contentment with what is.

Write down three or four statements about how you *thought* your life should be. Next to each statement, write down something that you like about the way your life is *now*. Find gratitude and acceptance in what is present today.

1. ____

2. ____

3. ____

4. ____

Let go of having to be right by reminding yourself that there is nothing that you have to prove to *anyone*. Do you want to be right or do you want to be happy?

Write down three or four things that you "know" you are right about. Next to each statement write down why it doesn't matter if you are right about it or not.

1. ____

____

____

2. ____

____

____

3. ____

____

____

4. ____

____

____

"Radical acceptance rests on letting go of the illusion of control and a willingness to notice and accept things as they are right now, without judging."

~ *Marsha Linehan* ~

Forgiveness, Mercy, and Acceptance

"When you hold resentment toward another, you are bound to that person or condition by an emotional link that is stronger than steel. Forgiveness is the only way to dissolve that link and get free."

~ *Catherine Ponder* ~

Forgiveness is a paradigm-shifting solution for transforming anger. It liberates us from the trap of endless resentment and desire for revenge so that we can experience more joy and connection. One doesn't need to believe in a universal, all-powerful being or even be religious to understand the positive influence and force that forgiveness can be in our lives. All too often people hold on to a grudge, a sense of frustration, or anger at a perceived or actual slight. Sometimes people hold on for many years when they could have forgiven long ago and enjoyed a greater sense of inner peace and freedom. Forgiveness is not only a beautiful feeling, but also good for our mental and physical health. Research conducted by the Mayo Clinic suggests that forgiveness helps us to move forward in a healthy way.

Also, forgiveness is generally thought of as emotionally letting go of resentment and thoughts of revenge. Forgiveness doesn't mean that you deny the other person's responsibility for hurting you; and it doesn't minimize or justify the wrong. You can forgive the person without excusing the act or inviting that person back into your life. Forgiveness brings a kind of peace that helps you go on with life.

"Forgiveness is the release of all
hope for a better past."

~ *Buddy Wakefield* ~

Forgiveness is a process that liberates the forgiver, not the perpetrator. Forgiveness is not about forgetting, it is about relieving the mind and heart of the emotional sticky tape that keeps us stuck, angry, depressed, and unhappy.

Forgiveness gives us wonderful gifts to nurture our minds, hearts, and spirits, including:

- Improved relationships
- Greater well-being, both spiritually and psychologically
- Less anxiety, stress, and hostility
- Lower blood pressure
- Fewer symptoms of depression
- Stronger immune systems
- Improved heart health
- Higher self-esteem

Forgiveness is our ability to let go and it is also a sign of personal growth. Sometimes we have a need to forgive others, but often we have a need to forgive ourselves. As humans, we can be strong and passionate, but we can also be fragile and vulnerable. We are all prone to mistakes, as that is part of the human condition. Yet, oftentimes we hold on to these mistakes as if they're more important than the sum total of everything else we've done in life. In this section we'll discuss ten ways to work on integrating forgiveness into one's life.

"The weak can never forgive.
Forgiveness is the attribute of the strong."

~ *Mahatma Gandhi* ~

The elephant in the room: why forgiveness is so hard

Forgiveness is often difficult for many, especially if there has been a great deal of trauma or other abuses in our lives. Sometimes, however, people choose not to forgive. We would rather hold on to negative thoughts or feelings about someone. There are some of us who believe that if we forgive, we are condoning or cosigning another's inappropriate or otherwise negative behavior. However, experts disagree. Universally, researchers have discovered that forgiveness does not mean condoning, excusing, forgetting, or denying an offense. It also does not have to involve reconciliation or putting yourself back into an abusive relationship.

One of the reasons some people find it hard to forgive is because their pride or self-esteem is injured. It can also be that expectations or dreams have been forsaken. There is a belief that something very valuable has been lost or taken, which leads to a desire for real or perceived compensation for the damages. Explanations for behavior can also get in the way. When someone is hurt, they can feel let down and assign rationalized causes for the behavior of others. Some will suggest that it is based on personality or character traits. So people tell themselves that others are forgetful, lazy, careless, unappreciative, mean-spirited, sick, unworthy, or purposely vindictive. This leads to judging someone harshly and lacks empathy for others.

Empathy is the ability to see a situation from another's perspective, to place yourself in their shoes. The inability to forgive can become emotionally and physically toxic. It can make us sick. Forgiveness is a powerful and positive journey for those who are ready and prepared to let go of their past hurt. However, this courageous healing step must be made at one's own pace and only when liberation from the suffering is the next desired step. Sometimes empathy for an abuser can be a trap that their victims fall into—like the "Stockholm syndrome." Therefore it is important to state that protective precautions as well as healing must occur before empathy can become a healthy emotional response that makes room for forgiveness.

Some people can become so vested in their anger, grief, sadness, and hard-liner approach to what happened in the past because they are receiving some sort of benefit or secondary gain from the misery. I call this the negative return on investment. The negative ROI is that we justify and use our pasts to define and legitimize our present misery, rendering us as powerless victims, absolved of any responsibility for life here and now, in the present. This emotional position guarantees unhappiness. It makes change seem too risky because by changing we are taking back control of our life from our familiar, unhappy self. This requires honesty about our role in the perpetuation of our own needless suffering. It also requires that we roll up our sleeves and get busy creating a new way of being that is a lot more productive as well as joyful.

The gift of compassionate self-forgiveness

Quite often the person we tend to judge most harshly is ourself. We fill our minds with doubts about ourselves: Why did I say that? Why do I make such poor decisions? Why did I get in that relationship? If only I could do better, etc. This tendency creates not only a sense of doubt about who we are and our capabilities in life, but it also generates low self-esteem and undermines our confidence. We then act in ways that justify our own negative expectations.

Psychologist Dr. Rudy Klimes offers the following 5-step process for granting the gift of forgiveness:

- **Acknowledge anger**: go ahead and admit all the emotions surrounding the situation: resentment, sadness, grief, frustration, and darkness. Forgiveness might not totally dissolve anger, but it will give us the freedom of knowing we are so much more than just our rage—regardless of its tendency to take control.
- **Bar revenge**: agree to eliminate revenge or getting even as a useful healing strategy. The ultimate justice lies in living well as the best revenge

by choosing happiness, creating success, and the triumph of not giving others any dominion over our peace of mind.

- **Consider the offender's perspective**: acknowledge that forgiveness refers to the actor, not the act. Not to the offense, but the "woundedness" of the offender, recognizing that s/he or the situation possesses its own complexities that need not hold us emotionally hostage.
- **Decide to accept the hurt**: Dr. Marsha Linehan, creator of Dialectical Behavioral Therapy (DBT) coined the phrase "Radical Acceptance," meaning we choose to wholeheartedly accept what has happened to us at the depths of our minds, bodies, and souls. We feel it. We feel a lightening, a release, and a sense of peace. We acknowledge our misery or consciously accept what has happened to us and find creative ways to move beyond our adversity and accept the realities of life.
- **Extend compassion**: compassion is an emotion created by placing one's self in the shoes of another. It is a sense of shared suffering mixed with a desire to reduce distress. It is a way of showing kindness, sincerity, and emotional alignment with another often characterized by actions of aid or nonjudgmental regard. Compassion is not pity or sympathy. Compassion connects us through the human heart. Pity and sympathy emotionally separates and distances us from one another.

During a recent Harvesting Happiness Talk Radio interview, my guest Dr. Joel Levey, cofounder of

Wisdom at Work, shared with me a fantastic exercise targeting enhanced empathy for another called "Oh, just like me . . . " It's actually more of a mindfulness practice designed to activate our humanity leading us to acknowledge that everything we desire for ourselves is desired, as well, by everyone else—including our perceived transgressors and trespassers. Here are some examples—"Oh, just like me, this person, who battered me as a child also just wants to be happy. Oh, just like me, this person who criticizes me really longs for peace. Oh, just like me, this person who betrayed my trust really wants to be appreciated." This acknowledges the plight of the human condition, softens our hearts, and allows us to extend compassion without compromising our own integrity.

Letting go and moving on

Our beliefs about forgiveness may also be either propelling us forward or holding us back. Some people are guided by their spiritual or religious beliefs. As such, they may wait until an appropriate time of year or ritual so that they can engage in the act of forgiveness. Whether we have these views or not, many people also have self-limiting beliefs around forgiveness. They may have convinced themselves that only legal reparations will suffice, or a verbal apology, or some other formal sign that the person who has "wronged" them understands and makes some sort of important apologetic gesture.

The challenge with this belief system is that the other party (person or group) may either have no idea that they have wronged someone, or they may have an entirely different view of the situation altogether. This creates a problematic situation, since one party wants

something the other party is unaware of or unwilling to recognize.

The mental journey around forgiveness is to check in with oneself and understand the importance of letting go of certain beliefs and judgments that you're holding on to. Why are reparations important? What would an apology achieve? Sometimes neither reparation nor apology is possible. Yet people hold on to to the belief that it's the action of another that will that will make the difference. But it's actually our own beliefs that need to be dealt with first. We have to ask ourselves, what is preventing us from engaging in the act of forgiveness? What can we do in our own lives to create a sense of closure for the situation? The fact that binds this together is that we can't control or force the actions of another. We can only govern and guide ourselves. It is ourselves that we must work with, rather than focusing on the behavior or acts of someone else.

Understanding why the past can haunt us and how to move forward

The issue of forgiveness is for events that took place in the past. However, one way to view this is that the past is done, the future is not yet created, and all we have is the present. Truthfully, if we are always living in and haunted by our past, then there is no way we can be living in the present. The well-known humanistic psychologist, educator, and author Dr. Carl Rogers created the person-centered approach to therapy, focused on the importance of the present. He did not suggest that past events were unimportant, but rather wanted to know how clients were affected in the moment. It is in the present where our efforts should focus because that is all we have today and where our certainty resides.

So, while we may have past issues to deal with, the question may be: "how are you allowing or choosing to allow the past to affect your present life?" To stay in the past is a choice. We can deal with our past, but still choose to live in the present.

A few tips for dealing with the past include:

- You can't change the things that happened in your life, but you can decide how you interpret and respond to them. If you didn't receive support when you needed it, give it to yourself now.
- Consider what you need to do to get emotional closure.
- There is no right timeline for recovery. For some people, making peace happens suddenly and spontaneously. For others, it takes time and effort. You may have to make a conscious effort every day to forgive.
- Don't cling to negative feelings. Anger is nothing more than an outward sign of hurt, fear, guilt, sadness, grief, or frustration. While the pain may never completely disappear, forgiveness can help you release the anger and bring those in your life closer to you.

The "walking wounded"—the battle scars of living and the combat gear we all carry

Fact of life—everyone has issues, everyone has problems, and to correct a cliché: the grass is NOT greener on the other side, even though we often imagine that is the case. How is this relevant to forgiveness? When

we look at our own lives, we often find it difficult to cope with some of our more challenging issues—relationships, finances, employment, past traumas, disappointments, and setbacks. There are no lack of problems facing the modern man and woman. But, whether we like to think of it in this way or not, everyone else is carrying the same problems. It can be very tempting to think that more money would solve everything, or a marriage, or a child, or the perfect job, etc. The likelihood is that these can enhance (or complicate) our lives, but not ultimately transform them.

As we move through life, our load will be a lot easier if we don't make the bag we have to carry over our shoulder heavier than it already is. The longer we hold on to grudges, the more people we feel negatively about, and the more we retain our negative emotions, the heavier that bag is going to become. It will bulge with the intensity of our frustrations. We can lighten our own load by learning to forgive and let go. The tools and practical strategies outlined in this book can help support you in easing the load of your baggage. Imagine how it would feel to remove the excess emotional weight off your shoulders that you have been carting around years in order to live a life of greater enjoyment and fulfillment.

Walking and growing through the stages of forgiveness

As with grief, there are stages of forgiveness. First, you have to acknowledge that you have to forgive. It is important to your psychological health. Carrying old wounds is simply a burden that steals the pleasure from the life that you could have now. We are not on this earth forever, and sitting in victimhood can be such a loss, not to mention repellant to those we love.

Acknowledging a wound that needs healing is only a first step. You also have to deal with real feelings of anger and at times, betrayal. The word FAIR is an excellent metaphor. Too many people can't get over just how unfair life is. Such pain, for what? Life does look unfair, but it is also filled with the potential for beauty, love, and grace. The anger over things having been unfair is a product of our immature minds needing to have justice. Yes, there may be a universal balance, influenced or supervised by some invisible energy or by nature, but it often has little to do with the narrative that we want to write.

So, the first step is acknowledgement. The second step is taking into consideration what you need to do to forgive. The third step is to engage in a forgiveness ritual or event of some sort, and the final step is to let go and have closure. Forgiveness is a process and NOT a destination. For some situations it will take longer. Each life is a course in life, itself. We are taught by our experiences and no textbook can really do it for us. Learn what each chapter has to teach you. Forgiveness is part of the parcel of the emotional work of learning these lessons well.

Forgiveness is an act of self-love

All too often people equate forgiveness with forgetting. They are not the same thing. When we force ourselves to try to forget something, it actually remains inside our unconscious mind. The memories fester inside of us and have the ability to cause us all kinds of emotional and physical difficulties. The images will likely play themselves out inside of our dreams. They

will also affect us in our waking life. For example, if one partner abuses another in a relationship and the two ultimately split, there can be forgiveness; but it is important to remember the lessons of the experience.

This is what forgiveness is:

- Making yourself responsible for how you feel
- An important contributor to your own healing. It's not about people in your life who have hurt you
- Learning to take wrongs less personally
- Becoming a victor instead of a victim in the story
- A trainable skill, just like learning to throw a baseball
- A choice

And, forgiveness is not:

- Forgetting that something painful happened
- Excusing or condoning the poor behavior
- An otherworldly or religious experience
- Denying or minimizing your hurt
- Necessarily reconciling with the offender
- Waiving the right to justice or compensation
- Changing the offender's behavior; even if you change, the other person might not
- Always easy

Letting go with grace—forgiveness rituals

Rituals of forgiveness can be a beautiful way to finally let go and move on. When we perform a ritual, we remind ourselves of the importance of the situation, but we also give ourselves permission to release old patterns and move forward in a more positive way.

- **Readiness**: there is no timetable for forgiveness. In fact, it is not even a requirement. Acceptance may be as far as you are willing to go. However, the ability to forgive is a hallmark of a healthy, well-balanced, mentally fit, grounded individual. And I dare say happy people, myself included, have found a way to make forgiveness a part of their emotional fitness. Why? Because it works to clear out negativity to make space for something more emotionally nourishing and satisfying.
- **Meditation and reflection**: the use of quiet time for relaxation and contemplation is a very gentle way to forgive. As with all meditations, one should find a comfortable space. Make sure the time is set aside and there will be no interruptions. Some people like music or chanting, while others prefer silence. The meditation can be a phrase you say in your head, or it can just be a time of soothing "mental relaxation." Gently remind yourself that when you emerge from the meditation, you will have begun the process of release and forgiveness with intention.
- **Write a letter or poem**: the act of writing down words is another powerful way of forgiving. You can write the letter to the person (or yourself); they may be alive or they may have passed on. Say what's in your heart. Say all the things you need to say. Don't mail the letter, but do something symbolic. Perhaps you burn it, tear it into little pieces and flush it down the toilet, toss it in a large body of water, or even bury it somewhere with spiritual symbolism.

- **Write or find a prayer**: here is where you can seek help from someone in a position of spiritual authority who may be able to assist you—either on-line or in person. A teacher, rabbi, priest, or other cleric may know of a wonderful prayer you can say. It might be nice to light a candle during the prayer time and let it burn for several hours after the prayer has been spoken.
- **Create a ceremony**: write down who and what you wish to forgive elaborating all the ways your thoughts, feelings, and emotions have held you back or kept you stuck. Perhaps the situation has kept you from meaningful relationships, or from achieving dreams and desires. Perhaps it has compromised your health or even kept you from creating a happy life. Create a process to permanently release and forgive by burning or shredding and flushing what you have written. Use your imagination to release what you are committing to no longer hold.

The impact of forgiveness

There is research taking place that demonstrates that forgiveness is not only emotionally valuable but physically beneficial, too. Forgiveness apparently touches us on the deepest levels of who we are. In study after study, results indicate that people who are forgiving tend to have not only less stress, but also better relationships, fewer general health problems and lower incidences of the most serious illnesses—including depression, heart disease, stroke, and cancer. Forgiveness research is a relatively new and exciting field that, along with other mind-body research, is encouraging a fundamental shift away from treatment of disease to focusing on the positive aspects of human nature as a basis for healing.

A second way forgiveness works is more subtle, as shown in studies indicating that people with strong social networks—friends, neighbors, and family—tend to be healthier and happier than loners. According to psychologists, someone who is angry and remembers every slight is likely to lose relationships during the course of a lifetime; while people who are forgiving are more likely to attract and keep a strong social support system—to the benefit of their own health and happiness.

Just breathe—forgiveness and stress management

First, forgiveness is good for your heart. Studies found forgiveness to be associated with lower heart rate and blood pressure as well as stress relief. This can bring long-term health benefits for your heart and overall health. Forgiveness can also help reduce other negative effects on our health such as insomnia, anxiety, panic attacks, emotional conflicts, fatigue, and other somatic complaints.

Forgiveness helps us restore emotional balance to our lives. We let go of the negativity we have been holding on to, and in doing so, we make our load in life so much lighter.

This is a simple equation:

FORGIVENESS = LESS STRESS
LESS STRESS = A HAPPIER LIFE

So, to sum it up, forgiveness is good for your mind, your body, your relationships, and your place in the world. That's reason enough to do the work of letting go of anger and focusing on forgiveness.

Forgive others who you think have wronged you because it makes emotional room for something better, including happiness. It is imperative to change the way you perceive the transgressor. No longer see them as the person who has the power to hurt you but as a person who is acting out of their own unhappiness. Muster up compassion for them, for they have not learned how to be happy. In most cases they too have been deeply wounded. Talk about what happened with your friends and family just enough so that you feel relieved. Then let it go and move on.

Name three or four people you feel have done some wrong to you and how. Next, adjacent to their name write one positive thing that they have added to your life. Perhaps this person did something good for you, or perhaps there was good that ultimately came out of the relationship despite the wounding that occurred.

Name: ______________________

____

____

____

Name: ______________________

____

____

____

Name: ____________________

____

____

____

Name: ____________________

____

____

____

Say, "I forgive so and so because I am choosing to replace that negative emotion with something greater for my highest good."

Forgive yourself for your flaws by accepting your own humanness and that no human is flawless. Absolute perfection does not exist, so give up trying to achieve it. We are all perfectly imperfect creatures.

Now write down three or four of your flaws. Next to each flaw write down "I accept this flaw. Others accept this flaw."

1. ____

____

____

____

____

____

____

2. ____

3. ____

4. ____

Forgive yourself for any perceived failures. Failures are merely opportunities for growth and an invitation to try again. If you tried, then you have succeeded at trying. Failures can be reframed as possibilities for learning and transformation.

Next, write down three or four of your failures again. This time write down after each failure "I forgive this failure. I succeeded in trying and learned something in the process."

1. ____________________

____

____

____

____

2. ____________________

____

____

____

____

3. ____________________

____

____

____

____

4. ____________________

____

____

____

____

Letting go also involves not clinging to past mistakes. Remind yourself that you made the best decision possible based on all the information, tools, and resources you possessed at the time and that it just turned out wrong. *Forgive* yourself.

Write down three or four mistakes you have made in your life. Next to each statement write down how forgiveness of yourself and your mistakes would help you achieve a happier life.

1. ______________________________

____

____

____

____

2. ______________________________

____

____

____

____

3. ______________________________

____

____

____

4. ______________________________

____

____

____

Let go of obsessive thoughts and worrying by using your energy to do everything you can do to fix a situation and then surrender it to your source (Higher Power, the Universe, God, etc.)—however you envision that.

It's time to write down three or four of the main things that constantly worry you. Next to each statement write down what you have done to solve the worry. Next to that, write down the sentence "I have done everything I can and turn this worry over to the source (Higher Power, God, the Universe, etc., or whatever practice you connect with)."

1. ______________________________

____

____

____

2. ______________________________

____

____

____

3. ______________________________

____

____

____

4. ______________________________

____

____

____

Let go of thoughts of revenge because they are negative, toxic, and perpetuate unhappiness. Do this by accepting that life is not always fair, happy, or righteous, and that creating your own happiness is the best reward.

Think about revenge and the role it's played in your life. Write down three or four thoughts of revenge that you may have. Next to each thought, write down how you are hurting the person from whom you seek revenge. (It is probably not hurting that person at all, though.) Next to that, write down how you are hurting *yourself* by having these thoughts of revenge. You might also consider how you might be hurting yourself or wasting precious time and opportunities in the process.

1. ____

____

____

2. ____

____

____

____

3. ____

____

____

____

4. ____

____

____

Let go of grief, judgment and emotional limitations concerning an abusive childhood or a dysfunctional family. Stop making it an excuse for not being able to control of one or more aspects of your life. Take responsibility for your own life, stop blaming your parents, and forgive them for their humanness if you truly desire to create a happier life for yourself.

It's time to admit something big! Write down three or four people whom you blame for your unhappiness. Next to that person's name, write down how you blaming them could be hurting them. (Again, it is probably *not* hurting them at all.) More importantly, next to that write down how blaming them is hurting *you* and impeding *your* happiness.

1. ______________________________

____

____

2. ______________________________

____

____

____

3. ______________________________

____

____

____

4. ______________________________

____

____

Let go of "would have, should have, and could have" by doing something positive to improve your life *now*. Regret always occurs in the rear-view mirror—it only appears after the fact and does not always do so with perfect clarity.

Write down three or four things that you "should have, should have, could have" done. Next to those statements, write down what you can do *now* to proactively make your life happier and feel better about yourself.

1. ____

____

____

____

____

2. ____

____

____

____

3. ____

____

____

____

4. ____

____

____

____

Let go of your fears by leaning into them. Fear is not the enemy. Fear is natural when we do something outside of our comfort zone. Instead of trying to eradicate fear, decide to work with it by practicing more courage. Do something that you have always feared. Stretch yourself because our greatest growth happens outside of our comfort zone.

Now, write down three or four fears that you have always had. Next to each fear write down what action you can take *now* to face that fear. Do it! Remember, we tend to grow and thrive when we are challenged by just enough "good stress" to trigger movement from the familiar to new territory.

1. ____

2. ____

3. ____

4. ____

Let go of your fear of dying by doing everything you can do to ensure your good health and safety.

Write down three or four reasons why you might die prematurely. Next to each reason, write down what you can do to lessen that chance. (For example: If you fear dying from cancer, write down stop smoking. If you fear a heart attack, write down start exercising. If you fear an accident, write down don't drink and drive.)

1. ____

2. ____

3. ____

4. ____

Next, write down this sentence: I will do everything in my power to protect myself, to keep myself safe and to support my good health and well-being at this time and then I surrender my fear to walk with courage and embrace life.

Let go of your fear of aging by taking good care of your body, mind, and spirit. Create a colorful and rich vision for your life ahead that includes goals both attainable and a few that may be a reach. The point is to do things you've always dreamed of doing in order to keep yourself vital, engaged, and looking forward to your next adventures—travel, take up oil painting, golf, or even writing a book.

Write down three or four things that you fear about growing old. Next to each fear, write down something positive that you look forward to doing when you are older.

1. ______________________________

____

____

____

2. ______________________________

____

____

____

3. ______________________________

____

____

____

4. ______________________________

____

____

____

There was a study done a few years back that revealed the older we are, the happier we may become. According to the American National Academy of Sciences, based on a survey of 341,000 people, enjoyment of life begins an upward trend in the late 40s and does not peak until 85.

Studies show that we start out pretty happy when we are young and that as we progress into adulthood our happiness dips bottoming out in mid-life. Happiness levels seem to rebound nicely in our later years. This forms what is known as a U-shaped happiness curve and there are several contributors to the phenomenon. When we are young we don't have much responsibility or pressure. As we progress into mid-life there are more demands on us and while they can bring tremendous rewards, it can also add burdens that bridle our joy such as child-rearing and financial stress. By the time most of us hit our late 40s or early 50s the children become more self-sufficient and our careers have become more stable, hence a rise in our happiness levels. As we age, we tend to be less concerned about materialism and ambition as well as more focused on our relationships and experiences. Additional gifts of our maturity are becoming less preoccupied with what others think and being more at ease in our own skin allowing us to more joyfully occupy our lives.

"True happiness comes from the joy
of deeds well done,
the zest of creating things new."

~ Antoine de Saint-Exupery ~

Let go of your addictions by finally believing that you *deserve* to be happy and healthy. Yes, unhappiness—also known as "married to misery"—is an addiction too.

Name three or four addictions you have. (It doesn't have to be drugs, alcohol, or food. It can be an addiction to negativity, the Internet, your cell phone, shopping—anything.) Next to each addiction write down what positive behavior can replace the addiction. If you cannot control your impulses and your actions compromise your daily life, well-being, and relationships you may in fact be a true addict. It might be time to admit you are helpless in regulating the substance or behavior and outsource support and treatment in service to your health and happiness.

1. ______________________________

____

____

____

2. ______________________________

____

____

____

3. ______________________________

____

____

4. ______________________________

____

____

Let go of "I'll be happy when" because tomorrow never comes and it is always today. This conditional state of being can be right now if you allow it. Do not postpone joy. It will not wait for you.

Put some thought into three or four things that you think will make you happy when they happen. Write them down and next to each thing, write down something about your life that makes you happy *now*.

1. ____

2. ____

3. ____

4. ____

Let go of professional pursuits that aren't working or a job that you no longer enjoy. Constructively focus your energy in creating a new business or finding a more agreeable job that does work to satisfy your financial needs as well as contribute to your happiness.

Write down three or four jobs, businesses, or projects that you would be happier doing. Next to that write down what you can do *now* to move forward toward that goal.

1. ______________________________

____

____

____

____

2. ______________________________

____

____

____

3. ______________________________

____

____

____

4. ______________________________

____

____

____

Let go of relationships that no longer work. Find new relationships that *do* work.

Write down three or four relationships that don't really work for you anymore. Next to each relationship, write down what you can do to resolve this source of unhappiness. (For example, you could choose to reframe your perception of that person, you could have a talk with that person, you could end your relationship with that person, or you can change the dynamics of your relationship.)

1. ____

2. ____

3. ____

4. ____

Find a way to see your life as a success despite any failures. Focus on what you've done right in your life, not on what you've done wrong. *Success is getting up one more time after you fail.*

Write down three or four failures that you *perceive* you have had. Now write down what you learned from each of these *perceived* failures. These are opportunities for growth and transformation.

1. ______________________________

____

____

____

2. ______________________________

____

____

____

3. ______________________________

____

____

____

4. ______________________________

____

____

____

Go back and cross out each failure—they weren't failures, they were learning processes.

Now write down three or four successes you have had. Next to each success write down how you can expand and leverage these successes in the future.

1. ______________________________________

____

____

____

2. ______________________________________

____

____

____

3. ______________________________________

____

____

____

4. ______________________________________

____

____

"Bring acceptance into your nonacceptance.
Bring surrender into your nonsurrender.
Then see what happens."

~ Eckhart Tolle ~

Transforming and Transcending Trauma

"I have been bent and broken,
but—I hope—into a better shape."

~ *Charles Dickens* ~

On the other side of the seemingly never-ending storm we call Post-Traumatic Stress is a rainbow of possibilities for Post-Traumatic Growth. This is the major focus of my practice—to help people find the deep core of happiness that resides within us all by transcending and transforming the sense of being irrevocably damaged.

Growth after traumatic and stressful events doesn't mean that we ignore what has happened but gain wisdom from it. Strangely enough, loss and distress are often necessary in order to experience the most amazing growth. One of the best qualities that can be developed or enhanced is that of resilience—a more prepared state of mind for any future traumatic events one might have.

Remember my earlier reference to the beautiful and highly relevant Japanese art form of *kintsukuroi*? It means "to repair with gold. This art form involves repairing broken pottery with gold or silver lacquer and understanding that the piece is more beautiful for having been broken and the history it possesses."

Stories of those who have grown stronger after tragic events have inspired and compelled us forever. We are always heartened to hear of the champion who overcomes seemingly insurmountable odds to rise again and create great value with their lives. We wonder how they did it. We admire their courage. In a way, we view them as superheroes—crusaders against the injustices that have been done to them. Individuals who have used personal tragedies to help others in need show us that within extraordinary trauma resides the potential for extraordinary transformation.

If you've been through something extremely difficult to endure, the most direct path through the darkness and suffering into healing and transformation is with the compassionate support of someone who has made this journey before you and can help you courageously dig deep within yourself to the part of you that truly is invincible. The gift of Post-Traumatic Growth is how it will help us make meaning out of our adversity, learn from the experience, and find new purpose in our life specifically because of it.

"The journey of the hero is about the courage to seek the depths; the image of creative rebirth; the eternal cycle of change within us; the uncanny discovery that the seeker is the mystery which the seeker seeks to know."

~ *Phil Cousineau* ~

Key #7: Treat yourself the way you wish to be treated

Be your own best friend. The trick is learning to embrace "In-Joyment". Your joy is already inside you. True happiness comes from within. When you treat yourself with the respect you deserve, you will attract the happiness you desire. The only way to cultivate the light that is within you is to treat yourself with honor, with grace, with kindness, with integrity, and with self-love. Then you cannot help but glow.

"If you contemplate the Golden Rule,
it turns out to be
an injunction to live by grace rather than
by what you think other people deserve."

~ Deepak Chopra, M.D. ~

The funny thing about happiness is that it is not about control. It is about consciously turning on your own internal lights and shining them out into the world to illuminate what is positive and right within your immediate universe.

Happiness begins when you admit to yourself that you deserve happiness in whatever form makes the most sense to you. While you might think you understand happiness right now, it's your commitment to the *H-Factor* that adds up to sustainable happiness and well-being. When we are mindful of the *H-Factor*, which we covered before Key #1, we are reminded of this: that which brings us happiness, increases our joy, helps us find our smiles, and makes our hearts sing is not fleeting/temporal happiness. We embody the *H-Factor* when we find ourselves enraptured by the moment we are in without regard to time, space, or external circumstances. It exists when we are in flow with our lives and are aware of how good it feels.

Many moons ago, I traveled around the world with my daughter, Kayla, to explore my hypothesis that every person, regardless of socioeconomic level, age, ethnicity, career, health, or life circumstances, possesses happiness or the means to feel happy. Together, we interviewed people from all walks of life—from religious leaders, politicians, inmates, and

actors to street vendors and the homeless—in an effort to discover the universal keys to happiness. The tangible result was my film, *H-Factor: Where Is Your Heart?* The most precious gifts from my filmmaking journey included watching the shifts in my daughter, soulfully connecting with the people we interviewed and witnessing my own metamorphosis as a seeker of the fountain of authentic, sustainable, and intentional happiness.

Even though you now understand what the *H-factor* is, it doesn't reside where you may think.

Can you discover the secret to the *H-Factor* in the latest self-help guide or by going to a therapist?

No, the *H-Factor* is not contained in any self-help book. Not even this one. It's explained in here, but only you can create it. It's not about processing negative emotions or past traumas; it's not about what your parents did or did not do.

Will you discover the *H-Factor* if you cleanse all the toxins out of your body?

No. You may feel better physically after a cleanse, but the *H-Factor* has nothing to do with a high colonic or juice fast.

Can a guru or teacher provide you with the keys to the big *H-Factor* secret by unlocking the mysticism and magic of the universe?

No. That would be moving in the wrong direction. The *H-Factor* isn't in the far reaches of the universe; it is in *you*.

You are the light and epicenter of your own joy. The secret to happiness resides within you. It is already there—just flip the switch and turn up the brilliance. Feelings of depression, oppression, and suppression are all a manifestation of repressing the light of joy within you. We came into the world happy and then the light within us was diminished by experience. In order to rekindle the light within, we must reawaken our inherent nature of joy.

Repression is part of the compression and contraction that limits our brilliance. When we live in a contracted state, we are coiled up and closed off to the greater life that is available to us. Conversely, when we live in an open state of mind and being, our consciousness expands. Our happiness already exists. We just have to find new ways to let it shine.

How do you do this?

- Make promises to yourself that you can keep.
- Do things that you actually want to do and that serve your growth.
- Be kind to your body and your spirit.
- Surround yourself with positive people.
- Remember your happiness first.
- Consider the feelings of others.
- Align your actions with your needs.

When you move through each day, you will move differently if you're happy. The moment you realize that you are the one who is responsible for your happiness, that you deserve happiness, and that happiness is your natural state, you'll treat yourself better and authentically feel more joyful. You will experience, in a word, "In-Joyment".

Starting right now, right here, accept nothing less than the best for yourself. How you define this is up to you. For example, if you're asked to go to a certain event and you really do not want to go, say "no" instead of "yes" (as you might have done in the past).

When you listen to yourself and treat yourself with respect, you will notice that you are better able to care for yourself and meet your own needs. You may already do this for everyone around you. Why not for yourself? Besides, the better you care of yourself, the more you will have to give to your friends, family, and the world at large.

Take the *H-Factor* challenge and treat yourself the way you know you deserve to be treated as a child of the Universe. It's the only way to tap into your inner light.

As we think about life's situations and scenarios, it is hard to imagine any of them being easier to manage or more joyful to be present in than those we take on with a sense of happiness and well-being in our hearts. Our minds are nourished and more creative when we embrace our humanness rather than condemn it. Strangely enough, many of us are more loving and forgiving to others than ourselves. Why? We all deserve to be treated with kindness. And in turn, our gift to the world is to extend that kindness outward.

Are you ready to commit to happiness by treating yourself well? Be an example of compassion, love, and self-acceptance for those around you. They will notice, they will be inspired, and they will learn! Let's start a kindness revolution, starting with how we treat ourselves!

"You yourself, as much as anybody in the entire universe, deserve your love and affection."

~ *Buddha* ~

Improving Mental Muscle Tone

These happiness exercises are designed to bulk up your emotional fitness and to help you focus on reprogramming your inner-thoughts so that you will feel more happy and positive.

1. Look in the mirror. Try to smile and think sad thoughts at the same time. Can't do it, can you? Exercise your smile muscles a bit each day, increasing the exercise time to 5-10 minutes more every day.
2. Step on a treadmill and crank it up to 4.0 mph. Turn up your iPod and try to walk fast or run on the treadmill and yet think sad thoughts. Can't do it, can you?
3. Blast some happy music in the car and then try to feel sad. Can't do it, can you? (Salsa music is my personal favorite.)
4. While driving in your car, alone preferably, put on one of your favorite CD's and sing along. No one can hear you, so you're safe if you can't carry a tune. Singing out loud makes you feel happier and it is impossible to feel sad. Try it!
5. Join a gym, take your dog on a daily walk, or take dance classes. Make a schedule that you will get

some type of enjoyable physical exercise at least 3 to 4 times a week. Stick to that schedule no matter what happens. Studies show that exercise puts people in a better humor, especially those whose spirits were the lowest before they started to work out.

6. Call one friend and make a concerted effort to sound and be upbeat. Make plans to meet that person and do something fun together. Each day call another person, even a new acquaintance. If you are feeling lonely, reach out to someone you may have just met.
7. Join a bicycle club, a hiking club, a church group, a book club, a car club, a board game club, or bridge group—any positive activity that gets you out of the house and redirects your attention from thinking about yourself and your problems.
8. Get out of your comfort zone and do something different. Sign up for a cooking class or an exotic vacation.
9. Write down three things that you would love to do but have been too afraid to do. Sign up to go ballooning, river rafting, or parasailing. Join a ski club. Take scuba diving lessons.
10. Participate more in life and get outside of yourself. Become a political or animal rights activist. Train for a "fun run/walk" , a marathon, or some event that stretches your body and mind . Reach out to meet new people and make more diversified friends.
11. When you get in bed every night, before you fall asleep, make sure you identify at least one exciting reason to wake up in the morning.
12. Program your dreams. Decide what you want to dream about before you go to sleep. Or pose a

question for your subconscious mind to answer while you slumber. Also set the intention to remember the dream and to receive clarity about an important issue.

13. Always go to sleep believing that when you wake up life will have a wonderful surprise for you. Believe it or not, you'll get that surprise.
14. Write down when something is bothering you. Then write down one or more ways that you can alleviate the problem in a positive way. Put the paper away for 24 hours. After 24 hours, take out the paper and either take the action you wrote on the piece of paper or throw the piece of paper away and decide to let go of what you wrote that was bothering you.
15. Write down each of your problems in one sentence only, each on its own index card. Then arrange the index cards in order of importance. For each problem, write down 3 possible solutions. Start by tackling the first problem. Decide which is the best of the 3 solutions and then do it. When that problem is solved, tear up the index card and throw it away. Go on to the next index card.
16. Write each problem on a separate piece of paper. Once you have solved the problem, put it in a flameproof dish and light it on fire and burn it.

"A successful man is one
who can lay a firm foundation
with the bricks others have thrown at him."

~ *David Brinkley* ~

Key #8: Happiness is an inside job

The source of your happiness resides in your reflection in the mirror. Polish what you see from the inside—out. Being mindful of what you are doing allows you to correct your course on the way to happiness. Happiness is an inside job. Happiness is *your* inside job. Promise yourself right now that you will become aware of negative thoughts when they creep in.

> "Find the place inside where there is joy,
> and the joy will burn out the pain."
>
> ~ *Joseph Campbell* ~

Each day, you get to make a decision: to be happy or not to be happy. Instead of feeling like you are a victim in your own life, you have learned that you are the one who calls the shots, the one who directs the traffic in your mind, and the one who creates happiness. You are, in fact, your own hero.

When you are active in creating happiness, things can go well. But because you've had many years of feeling that everyone else is to blame for your bad days, it might be easy (at first) to slip back into your old ways.

Notice when you're not as happy as you would like, and ask yourself these questions:

- What am I thinking right now?
- What am I feeling right now?
- What am I doing that isn't supporting my happiness?
- What action will I take to support my happiness?

These questions will put you back on track, and they will allow you to refocus your mind on what is positive and what is possible in your life.

The more you question what you're doing and how you're moving through your life, the more aware you will become of the times when you need to make a change to better support your happiness.

Every day is a lesson, and every day is an opportunity. How will you choose to show up for life?

Create a Happiness First-Aid Kit

In 2012, I had the great honor of participating in TEDxMalibu, a community-organized event created in the spirit of TED's mission of "ideas worth spreading," designed to spark conversation and connection. The theme focused on post-recessionary life and was called "Flourishing in the New Paradigm." I presented my talk entitled "The Inversion Theory of Joy" and unveiled the Happiness First-Aid Kit to wonderful reviews and feedback. Why? It's a simple, whimsical, lighthearted, and effective reminder that it is up to us to create our own happiness.

As you've seen so far, happiness isn't elusive. It isn't something that hides in the ethers waiting for you to accidentally stumble upon it. It is a choice. It is a way of life. And it can be harnessed using the steps we've already talked about. But sometimes, you need more than just a mental checklist of happiness theories. You need concrete reminders to help you connect with your happiness. Don't worry. I've got you covered. All you need is a Happiness First-Aid Kit, filled with everyday objects to guide you back to your happiness if you ever lose your way.

To create your Happiness First-Aid Kit, you'll need:

Mirror: to remind you that the change starts from within.

Chocolate: to remind you to eat dessert first—don't postpone your joy.

Bubbles: to remind you to connect with your inherent childlike sense of wonder to stimulate curiosity, enchantment, and delight.

Rose-Colored Glasses: to remind you that the way we view the world governs our attitudes and actions.

Package of Kool-Aid: to remind you that pure belief in yourself, which sometimes takes a leap of faith, turns into the sweet elixir of self-mastery. Sometimes, we just have to fake it until we make it.

Balloon: to remind you that we all have to expel our hot air from time to time yet have the potential to rise again.

Candle: to remind you of the light we all have within us.

A Packet of Seeds: to remind you that we can choose to cultivate joy at any time by planting the seeds, watering, and nurturing our personal well-being crop.

Once you gather your happiness symbols, put your Happiness First-Aid Kit some place where you can see it regularly. Create a special box or pouch to hold these and other meaningful symbols. When you

feel like you're veering off your happiness path, peak into your kit and find the remedy. Of course, a Happiness First-Aid Kit is a personal thing, so feel free to add to it.

So you now have all Eight Keys. You have your Happiness First-Aid Kit. You have some new awareness, tools, and strategies. You are well on your way to living a happier, more fulfilling life. But there's one more thing I can do for you: I'm going to give you five basic things you can implement on a daily basis to make sure you—and your happiness—flourish.

The Not-So-Secret Secrets

1. **Stay out of your own way.**
   Negative self-talk, doubt, judgment, fear, anxiety, and unforgiving behaviors are all spirit-killers and happiness-dampeners. When these feelings creep in, make a conscious effort to turn them off by focusing on something positive. Practice belief in yourself and the universe will follow suit.
2. **Appreciate what is right in your life while minimizing what is wrong.**
   Find the good in your life and exalt in it. Don't waste your strength envying others for what they have and you don't. Be as joyful for another's bliss, as you would for your own. Live in gratitude.
3. **Surround yourself with happy people.**
   Happiness is a positively viral contagion and has a lasting domino effect.
4. **Smile and make eye contact with others.**
   Connect with the universe. Let the world know your lights are on. Even if you don't see a smile on the face of someone else, give them yours.
5. **Pay it forward.**
   Do something nice for someone else. Practice random acts of kindness and you will expand

your joy and enhance the joy of those around you. Sharing is caring and its positive benefits last long after the act.

You have a plan! You have some skills to use. Are you ready and willing to feel happier?

Happiness is like a muscle. If we don't use it, we will lose it. We're all hard-wired to exist, but we're not necessarily wired to be happy due to the brain's focused priority on survival as well as our genetics and conditioning. And yet, the root of our very existence is joy. We all desire joy. At the core of the indomitable human spirit is the essence of pure joy. Life is not always easy and sometimes it dampens the light of joy that resides within us. The good news is that we can train for greater joy with the use of good tools and practice.

Attention + Intention + Action + Practice + Experience + Repetition = Harvesting Happiness

Happiness can be cultivated.

If you think about it, we don't need to be happy in order to survive. After all, we're animals, so survival is the most important thing, above all else. But surviving is different than thriving. And happiness is the potion that allows us to thrive physically, mentally, emotionally, and spiritually.

And that's why we need to refine and improve our skills, because happiness takes practice. First, figure out what makes you happy. Next, forget about what others may think. And third, invest in your happiness with your time, your spirit, and your light.

Remember to keep practicing your emotional fitness skills so they don't get rusty. In the hustle and bustle of life, it's easy to let your happiness take a backseat to your busy schedule or obligations. If you don't practice happiness, your capacity for happiness will suffer, like muscles that atrophy without use. By practicing solid self-care, you will nourish your mind, your body, and your spirit, and as a result, every facet of your life will benefit.

Many of us are worried about not being happy—but not many of us do something about it. That's because we look at happiness as something that is elusive and defined by fate. It's not. It's not something that's out of reach. Far from it. Happiness is something that you can learn, something you can refine, and something that you can *master*.

"There are only two ways to live your life.
One is as though nothing is a miracle.
The other is as though everything is a miracle."

~ *Albert Einstein* ~

Joy Generating

> "Through love all pain will turn to medicine."
>
> ~ *Rumi* ~

Here's some great advice: make love to life. Be passionate, be creative, be truthful, and be connected to it in every way possible. There is so much that we can do to improve our well-being—and it is within our control—to generate joy in our lives. This is by choice, not by luck or happenstance. Refuse to label yourself an unlucky person.

My work is greatly influenced by many disciplines, including: psychology, science, philosophy, spirituality, yoga, mindfulness, music, art, literature, mythology, and common sense. Georg Feuerstein, the founder-director of the Yoga Research and Education Center, wrote prolifically on the spiritual richness of yoga. In his essay, "The Deeper Dimension of Yoga: Theory and Practice," he explores the meaning of spiritual recovery. Influenced by this piece, I humbly offer my own spin with the addition of the emotional component to it:

1. We acknowledge that human conditioning, based on dualistic perceptions of good and evil, right and wrong, etc., is a stubborn and self-serving habit normally hidden from ourselves and others through denial. The root of our discomfort is self-deception and perception.
2. We become more curious about life and seek guidance supporting our efforts. We commit to cultivating new perspectives, embracing emotional hygiene, self-responsibility, and spiritual repair. In doing so, we begin to embrace the interconnectedness of all existence. The process is personal and methods vary from creating emotionally and spiritually supportive community to regularly consuming inspirational reading material and videos.
3. We initiate positive changes in our conduct that supports our commitment to new outlooks and ways of being in the world. Reading and talking about emotional and spiritual renewal are not enough. Action is required. "Walking the talk" by applying the principles we learn to all our activities and interactions demonstrates mastery and leads the way to lasting and profound change.
4. We practice compassionate self-forgiveness and understanding. We accept total and conscious responsibility for our awareness of automatic habits and reactions. We readily acknowledge where our perceptions may fall short of our new understanding of life.

5. We commit to undergo healing and purification required to shift our old outmoded thought and belief systems from negative, destructive, and nonproductive to a more stable, uplifting, and proactive outlooks and actions. We agree to replace egocentric habits of self-will, judgment, and separateness into more accepting and integrative attitudes.
6. We learn to show up for life with flexibility, curiosity, wonder, and delight so we can continue to learn, grow, and thrive through our new positive outlook.
7. We practice humility, empathy, and love in the midst of our process in order to become more emotionally and spiritually competent. Through this process we become more grounded and authentic as humans.
8. We assume accountability for what we understand about life and the principles of emotional and spiritual recovery. We apply this understanding to all relationships in order to create more healthy interactions and positive contributions in the world.
9. We integrate mental, physical, emotional, and spiritual well-being in our lives as a dynamic practice guided by our new proactive and productive outlook.
10. We cultivate real self-mastery and understand the true value of practicing discipline, self-regulation, and love in all matters, great and small.
11. We practice spiritual communion in ways that personally resonate as a means to know that we are not the center of the universe, but a part of a dimension of existence where we are all in-

terconnected. By doing so, we become more transparent to ourselves and insightful about our lives.

12. We open ourselves up to possibilities of radical acceptance and authentic bliss through transcending our past pain, suffering, and willful conduct. We transform those perceptions through self-honesty and paradigm-shifting consciousness. When we unhinge our ego-driven nature, we can fully recover our soulful essence and spiritual identity. Through this, we can come home to ourselves, more comfortably residing in our own skin. We become awakened and whole.

"I learned that opening myself to my own love and to life's tough loveliness not only was the most delicious, amazing thing on earth but also was quantum."

~ *Anne Lamott* ~

Recapping the Eight Keys to Unlocking a Joyful Life

Key #1: Life is tough, but happiness is available to us all.

Key #2: Your inner child is your inner sage available to guide you.

Key #3: More is not always better.

Key #4: We cannot control life, only ourselves.

Key #5: Our happiness is our personal responsibility.

Key #6: Choose activities and people that foster happiness.

Key #7: Treat yourself the way you wish to be treated.

Key #8: Happiness is an inside job. Happiness is your inside job.

You see, happiness is our birthright but not our entitlement. Each of us came into the world happy. It is human nature. Entitled to be happy? Who said? Entitlements are for those of us who believe we are owed something. Some outside source does not grant happiness to us. Happiness is ours to claim at any time and any place, regardless of external circumstance.

Remember: Attention, Intention, Action.
Practice. Experience. Repeat.

Parting Thoughts

"Comfort zones are where dreams go to die."

~ Lisa Cypers Kamen ~

When contemplating the optimal ingredients necessary for the recipe for a successful life I can't help but revert back to thoughts I've shared previously in the beginning of the book about the nature of the psychology of our inner lives and the parallel similarities of architectural design as it relates to the creation of physical space in our outer worlds.

In my first career I was trained to organize and design external physical space. The architectural design process begins with programming services to establish project goals and design criteria. This provides a rational basis for design decisions to ensure that the project accurately reflects the clients' values, culture, lifestyle, aesthetic goals, and budget while taking into account safety and technology. My partner, Christopher, likes to call this "spatial lawyering." The definition of a lawyer is a professional who advocates for and counsels clients to navigate unfamiliar matters related to a specialty. The architect provides similar assistance in creating physical space.

Questions an architect asks a client are deep and varied beyond simply what is the space intended for? This inquiry demands a very intimate approach to satisfying the most personal needs of the client. How is the cycle of life and its ever changing and evolving landscape to be accommodated? How does one want to feel in the environment—at ease, comfortable, relaxed, gracious, safe? How does one want to experience the space—directive and organized, experiential and organic? How is the space to be used and what are the clients' personal habits so that the environment can be custom-crafted to meet the needs, the vision, and the dream?

I believe our inner worlds are not much different. We evolve through life carrying the metaphoric baggage, books, boxes, and furniture that comprise our emotional lives. Depending on our experiences, our awareness, and our goals, we unpack our "stuff" in very different ways and times. Some of us are minimalists and we like to clear out the junk we are not using and some of us are hoarders holding on to every piece of paper we've collected. But most of us live somewhere in the middle, every once in a while we clean out some of the excess we can no longer carry but still hang on to much more emotional material than is necessary in order to feel satisfied, organized, and in control of our environments.

And sometimes we are so frightened of the haphazardly packed junk(our memories) stored in the attic (our minds) we ignore them completely until we realize that carting around all that "stuff" is hurting us and diminishing our happiness. And this is precisely what fascinates me about psychology as an "emotional lawyering" process used to design the life we want based on our needs, aesthetics, interests, lifestyle, and, ultimately, life cycle.

Fortunately, goal-oriented psychology, self-help, life coaching, personal growth, and transformation support are becoming more widely accepted as methods to facilitate designing and creating the lives that we wish to live. Outsourcing support for our mental health is slowly becoming destigmatized, offering everyone the opportunity to experience a better life and more happiness, regardless of our pasts and in spite of our challenges.

"Time does not change us. It just unfolds us."

~ Max Frisch ~

My question to you, dear reader, is what will you do with these keys to your kingdom of greater happiness and well-being? Consider spreading joy to others who could really use it now! Remember, happiness is about paying it forward and fueling the world's joy reserves.

As you move forward on your journey, I'd love to hear from you. Tell me about your experiences, your challenges, and your successes. Community is key and we need one another in order to thrive.

Each week I have the great pleasure of hosting *Harvesting Happiness* talk radio, a show that connects millions of listeners with motivating and influential agents of change who offer inspiring insights and practices to help us maximize our potential on the journey to greater happiness, well-being, and self-expression. I close each episode with the following heartfelt parting thoughts, which I extend to you as you continue your adventure of discovering greater passion, purpose, place, and meaning in your life:

> *Happiness is not a destination. It cannot be bought, sold, or traded. Happiness will never invite you to the party. Happiness simply comes down to a choice to show up each and every day in the world with passion, purpose, place, and meaning.*
>
> *Wishing you kind thoughts, kinder words, and the kindest actions. Until next time, remember that happiness is an inside job. Happiness is your inside job!*
>
> ~ Lisa Cypers Kamen

Gratitude Beyond Measure

I am immensely blessed and grateful to be surrounded by a tribe of staunch supporters who share my vision to make this world just a little bit brighter and more joyful place to live. To my family, I thank you for your unending love and standing by me through thick and thin. To my mentors, teachers, and colleagues, I am eternally grateful for your wisdom and insight that enhance my skills and fuels my tenacity. To my clients, readers, radio show guests, and listeners, I am grateful for your strength of heart, authenticity, and passionate persistence to find and share your happiness.

I am deeply appreciative to my friend and fellow author Rima Rudner for her immensely supportive insight, guidance, and resources.

Boundless gratitude to my global village that makes all Harvesting Happiness things happen—Caitlin Ryan, Andrea Minghelli, Rebecca Brayman, Sarah Stephens, Lili Hodgins, Ilanna Mandel; Steven Woodruff at Curious Monkey Marketing; Mariana Morales and Andrea Daly at Dogma Marketing; Cheryl Beatrice; Sandra Beck and her team at Beck Multimedia; my radio peeps Erik Anderson and Scott Frazier at Toginet.com; and Hans Laetz and the tribe at KBUU- FM 97.5 and radiomalibu.net. Without your enthusiasm, support, and trust in me, spreading my message around the world would not be possible.

Huge and limitless appreciation to the team that supported the birth of this book and made it come alive: Jill McKellan, editor and archive organizer, Laurel Airica, editor and word midwife that helped bind the manuscript together with love, Miladinka Milic the graphic designer got my vision of the glass of water and ran with it, Vladimir Zavgorodny who makes visual art by formatting written words, Patricia Spadaro for seeing all the nooks and crannies that needed TLC and coaching me into content consistency, and finally Nigel Yorwerth, my agent, for believing in the vision of harvesting happiness around the world.

From the fullness of my heart, I thank you all for your greatness and collaboration. Together we raise all ships.

Notes

Key #2

1. James Gorman, "Scientists Hint at Why Laughter Feels So Good," September 13, 2011, http://www.nytimes.com/2011/09/14/science/14laughter.html; Dr. Robin Dunbar et al, "Social laughter is correlated with an elevated pain threshold," http://rspb.royalsocietypublishing.org/content/279/1731/1161.

Key #3

1. Harold G. Koenig, "Religion, Spirituality, and Health: The Research and Clinical Implications," *International Scholarly Research Network—Psychiatry* 278730 (2012): 1-33.
2. http://greatergood.berkeley.edu/expanding gratitude.
3. Russell Grieger, PhD, "Happiness with Life 3: Practice Gratitude," *Psychology Today Blog,* November 30, 2014, https://www.psychologytoday.com/blog/happiness-purpose/201411/happiness-life-3-practice-gratitude.

Key #5

1. Walter Last, "Learning to Feel," http://www.health-science-spirit.com/learntofeel.html.
2. Barton Goldsmith, PhD, "Don't Bury Your Feelings," *Psychology Today,* November 4, 2013, https://www.psychologytoday.com/blog/emotional-fitness/201311/dont-bury-your-feelings.
3. Oliver Sacks, "My Own Life," *New York Times,* February 19, 2015.

4. Dr. Guy Winch, "How to Deal with Chronic Complainers," *Psychology Today,* July 15, 2011, https://www.psychologytoday.com/blog/the-squeaky-wheel/201107/how-deal-chronic-complainers.

5. Edie Weinstein, "Are You 'Addicted' to Complaining?" *Addiction.com Blog,* April 30, 2015, http://www.addiction.com/expert-blogs/are-you-addicted-to-complaining/.

6. Guy Winch, PhD, "Does Complaining Damage Our Mental Health?" *Psychology Today,* January 19, 2012, https://www.psychologytoday.com/blog/the-squeaky-wheel/201201/does-complaining-damage-our-mental-health.

7. Bernie Siegel, MD, "Remarkable Recoveries," http://berniesiegelmd.com/resources/articles/remarkable-recoveries/.

Photo by Frederic Charpentier

Lisa Cypers Kamen, MA, is an internationally recognized applied positive psychology coach, author, speaker, documentary filmmaker, and the creator and host of the popular radio show *Harvesting Happiness*. Lisa's global practice focuses on addiction as well as trauma and life-crisis recovery to help clients balance their minds, bodies, and emotions, create greater overall well-being, and transform Post-Traumatic Stress (PTS) into Post-Traumatic Growth (PTG). She is a frequent radio, television, and print media guest expert, TEDx presenter, and contributor to the Huffington Post, Positively Positive, and Inspire Me Today websites.

On *Harvesting Happiness Talk Radio,* Lisa celebrates personal growth and sustainable well-being through interviews with renowned and eclectic thought leaders, offering insight, inspiration, and tips for "harvesting happiness" even under life's most challenging circumstances. As the founder of the nonprofit Harvesting Happiness for Heroes, she spearheads stigma-free trauma recovery and post-deployment reintegration services for military personnel and their loved ones challenged by the invisible wounds of war. Her goal is to help them reawaken joy in their lives.

Other works by Lisa Cypers Kamen include the documentary film *H-Factor . . . Where Is Your Heart?*; *Harvesting Happiness for Heroes: Reintegration Strategies for Depression, Anxiety, Anger, Grief and PTSD*; and *Perspectives on Addiction: A Multi-Stepped Journey to Wholeness*. Lisa lives with her family in Southern California.

To learn more about Lisa and her work, visit:
www.harvestinghappiness.com
www.harvestinghappinesstalkradio.com
www.hh4heroes.org

Stay connected and in contact by getting social on:
Twitter: @LisaKamen
LinkedIn: Lisa Cypers Kamen
Facebook: Harvesting Happiness
YouTube: Lisa Cypers Kamen; Harvesting Happiness
Instagram: HH_TalkRadio
Pinterest: Harvesting Happiness with Lisa Cypers Kamen

"Spread love wherever you go.
Let no one ever come to you without leaving happier."

~ Mother Teresa ~
